thegoodwebguide

Parents

www.thegoodwebguide.co.uk

thegoodwebguide

Parents

Harriet Griffey

The Good Web Guide Limited • London

First Published in Great Britain in 2000 by The Good Web Guide Limited
Broadwall House, 21 Broadwall, London, SE1 9PL

www.thegoodwebguide.co.uk

Email:feedback@thegoodwebguide.co.uk

Original series concept by Steve Bailey

10 9 8 7 6 5 4 3 2 1

A catalogue for this book is available from the British Library.

ISBN 1-903282-03-9

Project Editor Michelle Clare

Design by Myriad Creative Ltd

Typesetting and additional design by Karen Brain

Printed in Italy by L.E.G.O. Spa, Vicenza

Acknowledgements

Many thanks are due to the team at the Good Web Guide, and in particular to Nicky Granville, whose contribution to the text and editing was invaluable.

And thanks, too, are due to my sons, Josh and Robbie, who tolerated my monopoly of the Internet with much forebearance. This book is dedicated to them.

Contents

The Good Web Guides

The World Wide Web is a vast resource, with millions of sites on every conceivable subject. There are people who have made it their mission to surf the net: cyber communities have grown, and people have formed relationships and even married on the net.

However, the reality for most people is that they don't have the time or inclination to surf the net for hours on end. Busy people want to use the internet for quick access to information. You don't have to spend hours on the internet looking for answers to your questions and you don't have to be an accomplished net surfer or cyber wizard to get the most out of the web. It can be a quick and useful resource if you are looking for specific information.

The Good Web Guides have been published with this in mind. To give you a head start in your search, our researchers have looked at hundreds of sites and what you will find in the Good Web Guides is a collection of reviews of the best we've found.

The Good Web Guide recommendation is impartial and all the sites have been visited several times. Reviews are focused on the website and what it sets out to do, rather than an endorsement of a company, or their product. A small but beautiful site run by a one-man band may be rated higher than an ambitious but flawed site run by a mighty organisation.

Relevance to the UK-based visitor is also given a high premium: tantalising as it is to read about purchases you can make in California, because of delivery charges, import duties and controls it may not be as useful as a local site.

Our reviewers considered a number of questions when reviewing the sites, such as: How quickly do the sites/individual pages download? Can you move around the site easily and get back to where you started, and do the links work? Is the information up to date and accurate? And is the site pleasing to the eye and easy to read? More importantly, we also asked whether the site has something distinctive to offer, whether it be entertainment, inspiration or pure information. On the basis of the answers to these questions sites are given ratings out of five. As we aim only to include sites that we feel are of serious interest there are very few low-rated sites.

Bear in mind that the collection of reviews you see here are just a snapshot of the sites at a particular time. The process of choosing and writing about sites is rather like painting the Forth Bridge: as each section appears complete, new sites are launched and others are modified. When you've registered at the Good Web Guide site (see p.142 for further details) you can check out the reviews of new sites and updates of existing ones, or even have them emailed to you. By using the disc at the back of the book or registering on our site, you'll find hot links to all the sites listed, so you can just click and go without needs to type the addresses accurately into your browser.

As this is the first edition of the Good Web Guide, all our sites have been reviewed by the author and research team, but we'd like to know what you think. Contact us via the website or email feedback@thegoodwebguide.com. You are welcome to recommend sites, quibble about the ratings, point out changes and inaccuracies or suggest new features to assess.

You can find us at www.thegoodwebguide.co.uk

User Key text

UK / US	Country of origin
£	Subscription required
R	Registration required
🔒	Secure online ordering.

Introduction

In many ways there's probably never been a better time than the beginning of the 21st century to be a parent. That said, it still remains one of the most challenging jobs known to woman and man, requiring the sort of resources and abilities traditionally associated with running the United Nations. It's a big job, and every year around 60,000 babies born in the UK ensures that an ever - increasing number of parents also come into existence.

We all do it differently, but we all share one thing in common: care of and commitment to our children. And although parenting can't ever be an exact science, it contains a number of certainties - one of which is that babies are born, grow up and become young adults, making it a constantly changing landscape. What parents need, as they make this journey with their children, are different things at different times in order to do this challenging job. Sometimes hard facts are needed, sometimes the support of knowing others have experienced similar problems and found solutions. Sometimes it is as simple as finding the perfect gift in two days flat!

Parenting comes with no job description or training, but requires you to become an overnight expert on all subjects ranging from pre-conception vitamins to immunisation schedules; educational toys to schools' league tables; meningitis symptoms to drug abuse; homework projects to safe surfing on the net. And that's where one of the big benefits of parenting at this point in history comes in - the internet, and its ever expanding source of websites.

The range of accessible information is already vast, and that alone can make finding the most useful sites difficult, which is one of the downsides of the net - when you don't know where to look. It's perfectly possible to spend ages trying to find one piece of information, but when you do know where to look, then the internet becomes a valuable friend.

Although not foolproof, the net has a lot to offer busy families and the purpose of this book is to enable parents and their families to use it to their best advantage. You could say that the net is a good servant but a bad master, so it's worth cutting through the technological hype and making it work for you as a resource of benefit and value. The aim is, in effect, to allow parents to see the net as a worldwide library of information, while avoiding the need for endless time - wasting searches. It also means you can learn to use the net's facilities with confidence, and pass on these benefits to your children, while being aware of both the net's potential and its limitations.

But it's not all sense and sensibleness. One big benefit of the net is that it can be fun giving you insights and opportunities via some of the sites that are inaccessible anywhere else where else could you check out the contents of the Louvre without going to Paris? One of the joys of parenting, so easy to miss in the day - to - dayness of family life, is the opportunity to experience and share with children the things that make life exciting. As many of the sites are designed to be entertaining as well as informative, the net contributes to this aspect of family life as well.

Going online might seem daunting enough in the first place, and once there it can be difficult to know where to start. As much of parenting can make you feel pretty much the same, knowing whether or not there's a site to meet your needs in the first place, and how to get to it, can be very reassuring. Broken down into broad categories, and selected for its contribution to each category, the site entries in this book are designed to give you a quick review of their contents. Many more sites than those included obviously exist, and many sites have extensive links to other sites, but this selection is based on their usefulness and value to busy parents.

Suffice to say that as journalist, and the mother of two children aged five and 14, my professional choice is tempered by my personal experience, but probably to its advantage. As a result I now have access to the information and resources I needed when, as a parent, I first started to surf the net! And now, with a foot in the internet door and new sites emerging all the time, I know that I am better equipped than ever.

Harriet Griffey March 2000

Chapter 1

Parenting in General

Parenting is a wide ranging subject which runs across different age groups, and these sites are selected for the diversity of general information they offer on the subject. Some sites are quite specific and others more extensive: they vary from single expert resources to full blown magazine style approaches. And as parenting usually involves a relationship of sorts with a co parent, due emphasis is given to this within numerous sites. In addition, while parenting never occurs in isolation it can make many parents, often mothers, feel quite isolated. Many sites also recognise this and provide discussion forums, message boards and chat options in order to provide that important contact with other grown-ups.

www.ukparents.co.uk UK Parents			
Overall rating: ★★★★★			
Classification:	Magazine	**Readability:**	★★★★★
Updating:	Regularly	**Reliability:**	★★★★★
Navigation:	★★★★★	**Speed:**	★★★★
UK R			

Billed as a monthly e-zine, UK Parents is essentially magazine-style in format, but interaction is encouraged at every level, from keeping your own on-line diary, to participating in forums and competitions. If you register on the site, each return visit or contribution can earn you Loyalty Points, which may make you eligible for a prize if you accumulate enough.

It is a well-designed site that's easy to use, with the benefit of a full site index. If you're looking for something specific, enter a keyword in the Search box or browse through the topics in the archive. Clear navigation tags across the top of the page help you move from section to section, and there are further links at the bottom of most pages if you scroll down.

If you get stranded in an article (most common in the Archive section), use the back button on your browser to return to the previous page. In the Forum section, use the Next link at the top of the page to follow the replies to a posting.

SPECIAL FEATURES

Archive A wealth of articles organised into sections such as Preconception, Your rights and Your Money, Pregnancy, Breastfeeding and Women's Health, Vaccinations, and sections dedicated to problems associated with children of particular ages.

The Daily Parent is the magazine part, updated daily, with Hot News, Horoscopes, News Express, Competitions, What's On, TV Pick, and more.

Charities and Help Groups is an excellent, comprehensive list of support organisations, complete with Links page to charity websites (from the Anna Freud Centre to the National Childbirth Trust).

Online Shops focuses on companies that provide mail-order services of interest to busy parents with too little time to shop with links to amazon.co.uk, Blooming Marvellous, The Original Gift, and more.

Forum is the place to explore topics and exchange ideas with other parents. It seems to act as a jumping off point for making e-friends!

Meet the team section is a very reassuring résumé of all the staff members, with editor Helen Humphreys, Dr Robert Welch (neonatal paediatrician), Alison Wall (health visitor) and Claire Preston (financial writer).

Other features

These include Links, a list of companies and organisations who have advertised or featured on ukparents (with free listing for non-profit making organisations)

At the time of review a complete overhaul of the site was promised and a move to new servers was causing a few problems. For the latest update, see the review section on www.thegoodwebguide.co.uk.

Chatty and friendly in style, this site is a particular boon for parents of under 5s who want either reassuring, down-to-earth advice or to make contact with parents sharing the same experiences.

www.telegraph.co.uk

The electronic Telegraph online newspaper

Overall rating: ★★★★

Classification:	Newspaper	**Readability:**	★★★★
Updating:	Daily	**Reliability:**	★★★★
Navigation:	★★★★	**Speed:**	★★★★

UK R

This is the online version of The Daily Telegraph newspaper, providing easy access to designated sections, which include those in this review - Schools, Teenagers, Students - within its front page menu, both at the top of the page and at the bottom. Because it is a newspaper site, with a search option, there is also the possibility of checking out general features and news stories of interest to parents. You need to register to use this site by filling in a simple form but this is free and provides access to all aspects of the site after that.

SPECIAL FEATURES

Schools section, described as providing 'a support site for the education community from the Electronic Telegraph'. This breaks down into main sections: Home and News - with a weekly review of news stories relevant to education; Virtual School - providing comprehensive lesson plans for Year 7 students, complete with accompanying notes for teachers and parents, and a directory of online schools throughout the UK; Guide to Educational Websites is updated weekly, and these are sub-divided into 17 different sections including history, english, science, art and design, music, geography, modern languages, maths, and teacher/parent resource sites; News in Action archive is a collection of historical and contemporary articles from the Telegraph, selected by teachers for their relevance to the Curriculum (for example, go to History, World War 1, to find the article written on 26 April 1915 about the Battle of Ypres); and finally, Global Forum which provides the space for an opportunity to communicate with students and teachers around the world... although not many are currently utilising this resource.

Teenagers T2 online features The Telegraph's weekly teen newspaper, published on Saturdays. It is available online in either 'shocked' (for which you need Shockwave Flash Plug-In) or 'non-shocked' versions. You can get both the current and the previous editions of T2 online. This magazine contains features on celebrity interviews, competitions, puzzles, a style section, sport, news and features (How I survived no TV for a week, for example), plus weekly e-polls on which you can vote (for example: Who is Beckham's boss - Alex or Posh?).

Students section is called Juiced. It is again a magazine complete with This Week news and features as well as film reviews, music reviews, and articles on sport, travel, fashion and careers. Celebrity Gossip content is provided by Heat magazine.

The Schools section benefits greatly from the input and accessibility of the Telegraph newspaper's education correspondent, John Clare, making this site a good resource for students, parents and teachers alike. The designated T2 and Juiced sites are also of excellent value for teenagers and college students.

www.educationunlimited.co.uk/parents/ The Guardian Newspaper			
Overall rating: ★★★★			
Classification:	Newspaper	**Readability:**	★★★
Updating:	Daily	**Reliability:**	★★★★
Navigation:	★★★★	**Speed:**	★★★
UK			

This is the parenting section of The Guardian newspaper's education section. Because of its weekly education supplement and also its weekly Parents feature, the newspaper has a wealth of past articles and special reports, plus a Talk option for those who have registered. However because the emphasis is very much on Education issues, a fuller review appears under the Education section of this book.

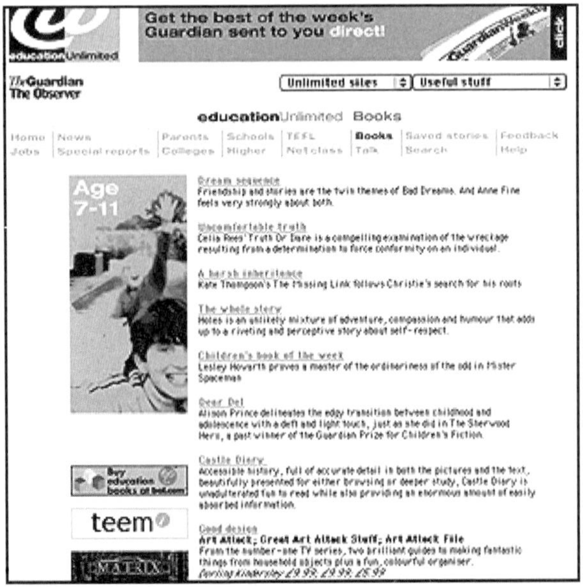

There is a good Children's Book section with a list of recommended reading in four categories by age: 0-3, 3-7, 7-11 and 11+ (however, 3-7 seems a very large range from those who cannot read at all to those who can). There is also a children's book of the week with a detailed review and you can buy online via BOL.com.

www.abcparenting.com ABC			
Overall rating: ★★★★			
Classification:	Magazine	**Readability:**	★★★★
Updating:	Regularly	**Reliability:**	★★★
Navigation:	★★★	**Speed:**	★★★
US			

This comprehensive index site has reviewed thousands of sites of interest to parents, and given them marks out of five plus a brief description of their contents. You can either click on the subject of interest on the homepage (options include Caring for Children, Education, Family (Genealogy, Travel and Fun), Health and Parenting) to see a list of relevant sites or search by a keyword. The latter facility wasn't in operation at the time of a first visit, though it worked subsequently - but that's the internet for you! The preponderance of banner advertisements can slow down the loading, but overall the site works quite quickly. Inevitably for a links site of this size, some of the links don't work, but there is such a wealth of articles here that the odd one doesn't matter too much.

SPECIAL FEATURES

The recommended links are the heart of this site, but ABC is part of the ParenthoodWeb family of websites and you have direct access from the home page to the following associated facilities:

Articles The current ones are listed in a box on the left hand side of the home page.

Discussion boards divide into General Discussion and Pregancy Discussion groups. You need to register to post messages.

Chat provides a well-organised schedule of chat sessions for all interests throughout the day (and the night - for when else do parents get any time to themselves?), but you need to add on eight hours to the listed times if you're a UK user. You will also need Javascript and Frames enabled within your browser, and you must install their ichat plug-in software, which can be downloaded from the site.

Other features

Links to experts who have listed information on the site; for example, the doctor who wrote the feature on whether or not children should have flu jabs can also be accessed direct via his website. Shopping is of limited interest to the UK user, but by following the link you'll get to a whole section on Sleep (what parent can resist?). And for those of an astrological bent there's a Parent-Child compatibility Chart!

A good place to start if you want to research a particular parenting topic and want to screen out the dross.

www.awareparenting.com

Aware Parenting Institute

Overall rating: ★★★★

Classification:	Organisation	**Readability:**	★★★★
Updating:	Regularly	**Reliability:**	★★★★
Navigation:	★★★★	**Speed:**	★★★

US

A website for the Aware Parenting Institute in California, based on the work of Aletha Solter, PhD, a developmental psychologist who studied with veteran child development expert, Jean Piaget. As a philosophy, Aware Parenting proposes an approach to raise children 'who are bright, compassionate, competent, non-violent, and drug-free'. The site covers topics from birth to adolescence, mainly in the form of articles, ranging from opposition to the use of Ritalin for ADHD to the principles of learning and what to do if a baby cries. Dr Solter's approach is based on attachment-style parenting, non-punitive discipline and emotional release work with infants and children. She has been working with parents since 1978, and no doubt her work provides a degree of emotional release for parents! The simple site construction and clear buttons on the home page mean moving around the site is quite easy. No prizes for design, but it does the job clearly and quickly.

SPECIAL FEATURES

Principles gives a brief rundown of the Aware Parenting philosophy, and is a quick way to find out if the approach is likely to appeal to you.

Articles includes extracts from Dr Solter's books and links to her monthly advice column for www.ParenthoodWeb.com (see p.28). Lots of sound advice here and the 20 Alternatives to Punishment is particularly useful if you often find yourself locked in a battle of wills with your child. Some of the articles are available in French and German, as well as English.

Links to other sites with related information. There are also direct links to selected, although not endorsed, organisations for the following subjects: Birth (six sites), Attachment Parenting (five sites), Non-punitive Discipline (six sites), Emotional Release, Listening and Healing (sixteen sites), Education (three sites) and Journals (seven sites). If, for example, you are interested in alternative education, the Continuum Concept, or Dr Arthur Janov's Primal Therapy, the links are there.

Other Features

Books If you want to read more, Dr Solter's three books are only available by order form faxed or mailed with payment – they are not available to buy online. Consultations can be made via email, phone or letter, or personal appointments are also possible for those living close enough to Dr Solter's home in the States! Details of Workshops are given if you want to move on from acting to doing.

This is a fascinating site for anyone wanting to find out more about child-centred parenting. It's worth checking out the site for the links alone.

www.family2000.org.uk

Jill Curtis

Overall rating: ★★★★

Classification:	Personal	**Readability:**	★★★★
Updating:	Frequently	**Reliability:**	★★★★★
Navigation:	★★★★	**Speed:**	★★★★★

UK

This is a single-expert site of the psychotherapist and writer Jill Curtis, a specialist in family issues. There are individual pages (with links) directed at parents, stepparents, grandparents, single parents, and gay and lesbian families. The site is an advertising-free zone and it is quick and easy to move around: the links to the sections appear on the left-hand side of every page.

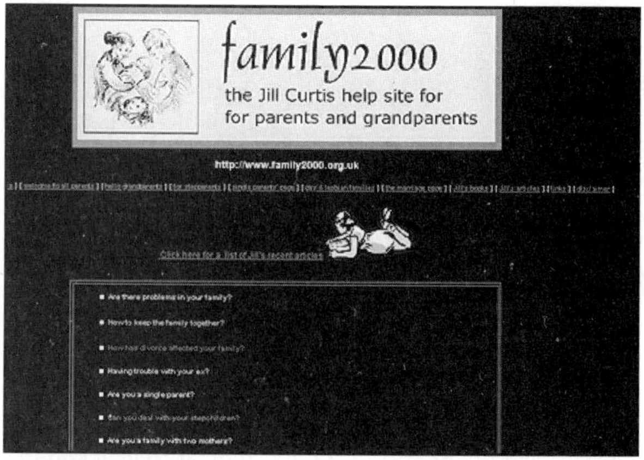

SPECIAL FEATURES

Jill's Articles Although there's no search facility you can scroll through the list of articles that that Jill has written for magazines, and then read them online (it may be quicker to print the longer ones and read them offline).

Jill's Books give you more details about her books, Where ís Daddy? and Making and Breaking Families, with links to amazon.co.uk to buy these.

Email Jill encourages email communication from her readers and is very generous in her responding. To contact her you can click into an email form from either the Welcome to All Parents page or About Jill Curtis.

A very straightforward site (and none the worse for that) covering the work of one expert and dispensing sound, down-to-earth advice.

www.handbag.com

Handbag

Overall rating: ★★★★

Classification:	Magazine	**Readability:**	★★★
Updating:	Weekly	**Reliability:**	★★★★
Navigation:	★★★★	**Speed:**	★★★★

UK

This is a very large site containing an enormous range of information, features, articles and magazine content. It appears to be targeted at women in a very general sense and some areas are better than others, for the purposes of this book we have checked out and recommend the education and family areas.

The website home page gives a good overview. The left side has a very long contents list with eighteen channels including the familiar (Arts & Entertainment, Education, Family, Fashion, Food & Drink, Health & Beauty, Home & Garden, Shopping) to less obvious (Careers, Local, Property, Tech Centre). These are always available on a pull-down menu on the top left corner of the page. There is then a further contents list entitled Accessories which contains the more peripheral areas such as Address Book, Chat, Discussion, Free Email, Horoscopes). You may find that the more you look at the site, the more confusing it becomes because several of the headings on each channel lead back to another channel. For example the 'highlights' panel sometimes had an expert answering questions and sometimes was announcing a new special offer – when you click on this you are taken back to the shopping channel.

Education channel divides into preschool, primary, secondary and university. It also includes The University option and has useful links to StudentUK, Student World, Universities and Colleges, and the Admissions Service (UCAS), plus links to drugs information services. The Primary section links to the Guardian eduction website. Otherwise, a good selction of articles on a range of subjects.

Family channel gives a wide variety of features. You can browse a virtual art gallery and search other excellent site links for kids. There is also information about a new meningitis test. The Discussion forum provides masses of advice, mainly from other mums. It is often supportive, but sometimes just an airing of views, for example on the subject of sex education at school. This is a great general section for parents and one of the more informative areas of the website.

SPECIAL FEATURES

The channel 'home-pages' of Education and Family have the following:

Today short descriptions of today's featured articles, probably around 6 on different but relevant subjects. On the day of being reviewed, the Education home page was including articles by a mother of a child with cerebral palsy, an article on bullying, and an article on saving for private education amongst others.

Highlights this is sometimes meet the expert but today on Family contained a review of Toy Story 2 and an article on fertility and drug use. This was actually an answer to a question, answered on a Science Line page, along with other relevant science questions, and which links the Family and the Education channels.

Ask Our Experts on the Education channel connects to the science line option whereas the Family section has a good range of parenting features from Dr Chris Brown answering questions submitted on pregnancy problems.

Business Finder: a database searchable by type of business

and area, provided by BT's Yellow Pages, but very general. For example on the Education channel a search for 'Nursery Schools' in 'London' gave a long list but did not include at least three I knew about. Like Yellow Pages, it just gives address and telephone number information.
Vote: a question for each channel with a click box to vote, a useful way of gaining information. The Family channel vote today was 'How much would you spend on family entertainment per week' with a choice of answers: 'up to £20', 'up to £30' and 'over £30'.

Other features

Each channel includes Offers (special offers), Competition (changes regularly), Shopping (takes you back to the shopping channel) and Quiz (several pages of trivia questions, just for fun)

Other channels of particular interest and with good, in-depth information are:

Chat features weekly lunchtime chats, with a designated 'expert' on Thursdays plus other times – details are posted ahead of time.

Address book feature where you can create and store your own address book system in cyberspace in case you lose your address book! You can also import your electronic address book by sychronizing from a Palm Desktop, Netscape Navigator, Microsoft Outlook and more. The advantages of creating an address book on this site include sharing contact information with friends, having up-to-date addresses all the time and being able to access it from anywhere in the world.

Links to other sites: Direct links to the site advertisers (for example, to Orange), but also to sites related to article subjects where appropriate.

Extensive general site, magazine-y in style, but strong on content for Education and Family sections and worth a look.

You do feel however that a lot of the content such as the quiz, competitions, links to other areas on the site, is just there to encourage you to stay on the site longer at each visit, and rather distracts you from the more useful in-depth areas.

www.myparentime.com

My Parent Time

Overall rating: ★★★★			
Classification:	Organisation	**Readability:**	★★★
Updating:	Weekly	**Reliability:**	★★★★
Navigation:	★★★★	**Speed:**	★★★★

US

This is a US-based site with direct link to the Stop Sex Offenders website (which, in turn, is linked to a US-neighbourhood crime check facility). This is a directory of a wide variety of sites of interest to parents, listed by subject which include Pregnancy, Parenting and Family, At Home, at Work, Health, Educational, FUN is fundamental, College Information and SeniorSpot. The home page has a monthly area with a new article (this month 'corporal punishment in schools'), a new poll (this month 'do you agree that corporal punishment should be allowed in schools?'), discuss (current monthly article and other topics). Although this is a thoroughly US directory, there is quite a lot of general interest information. For example, the White House website is listed under Educational.

SPECIAL FEATURES

Resources is an extensive list on the right side of the screen with a wide range of topics such as Site Map, Discussions, Free Pregnancy and Planning Software (link to Babyserv.com), Fun & Games (updated weekly – around 15/20 games at one time), Online Typing Test, Helpful Calculators (a long list of tables and calculators some useful to those living in the UK (Metric/Standard measurements, Body Mass calculations), some only to US residents (Driving Distance between Cities, Tax Calculator), Greetings Cards, Parent Pals, Missing Kids, and Contact Congress which are mainly available via links.

Features covers a news area, an article list, child safety information, pregnancy, parenting and family, an educational area. All these are links to outside websites rather than information being available on this site. Each subject gives a comprehensive listing of sites. For example, Colleges and Universities links you to websites for colleges and universities around the world, literally.

Stop Sex Offenders! This is an important link to their website where you can check (in the US only) your state's registry of sex offenders to see if any are around near you.

Discussion forums which cover pregnancy, parenting and STOP! Sex Offenders but at the time of reviewing only 28 members were registered and the last posting was a week ago.

Babysitter checklist This gives hints and tips on organising babysitter/childcare in your home. There is a very detailed checklist which you can print out and keep and includes the obvious emergency numbers as well as the more obscure such as the 'poison bureau'!

This is primarily a link-based site with all information provided by links to other sites. In addition, many of this site's sponsors, from enews.com to headhunter.com, provide a direct link. There is also shopping online links under category (such as Children, Books, and so on).

Although it can't be exhaustive, primarily because it is US-based, this directory makes an excellent first stop for finding a more specific website. Each listing is run with a short, informative paragraph.

www.parents.com Parents			
Overall rating: ★★★★			
Classification:	Magazine	**Readability:**	★★★★
Updating:	Daily	**Reliability:**	★★★★
Navigation:	★★★	**Speed:**	★★★
US R			

This is essentially an online version of the popular US magazine Parents, published by G & J USA group. It is well-organised and it benefits over its print counterpart in having easily accessible reference to further information articles within the site. Like most magazines of this type it has the usual mix of topics relevant to pregnant and new mums, and caters for children up to around five years. It is well-organised with features on the usual areas of interest, such as pregnancy and child development, food, living, fun and travel. You have to register to enter this website (or you can browse as a guest).

SPECIAL FEATURES

Ask the experts but note that replies can take two weeks. There is an impressive list of experts, covering obstetrics/gynaecology, paediatrics, and behavioural and clinical psychology, as well as a chef, nutritionist and a 'travel mom'.

Bulletin board is active – but registration took a long time as you are required to give lots of information to establish a personal home page.

Links There are lots of shopping links which are only relevant to the US. The recommended reading section is linked to Barnes and Noble's on-line bookshop, bn.com. Some of the experts have links to their own sites (for example, the paediatrician Dr Paula has a link to her own website at www.drpaula.com).

Although US-based, there is much of interest here for parents particularly if you want to ask the experts a particular question.

www.practicalparent.org.uk Practical Parenting			
Overall rating: ★★★★			
Classification:	Information	**Readability:**	★★★★★
Updating:	Regularly	**Reliability:**	★★★★
Navigation:	★★★★	**Speed:**	★★★
UK R			

This is a general parenting, UK-based site which is not related to IPC's Practical Parenting magazine. It was developed by Dr Andy Gill (PhD in psychology) as a resource and advice service for parents or carers of children under eight, and also for professionals and practitioners working in this field. It has a well-organised home page with easily accessible options.

SPECIAL FEATURES

Parenting Groups Research information about running successful parenting training groups, of interest mainly to professionals I would imagine.

Parenting Tips such as dealing with behaviour, looking after yourself and frequently asked questions (FAQs) about general parenting issues such as dealing with children's behaviour problems.

Practical Parenting Newsletter Subscribe to this free fortnightly newsletter. Registration is via Onelist (a long and tedious four-page form) after which it is difficult to get back to the home page.

Monthly Star Book Choice (in association with amazon.co.uk) with a review and a link through to amazon to buy on-line.

Parent-Child Game Challenge is a free 5-week online course for parents experiencing everyday child behaviour difficulties.

Other features

These include direct email to Dr Andy Gill at AndyGill@Freenet.uk.com. The response time is quick. There is also a chat room with clear instructions how to join (though the server was slow).

There are a few links, for example, to amazon.co.uk for book sales, also to netparenting.com, family2000.org.uk, plus a direct links resource section.

Information is limited but good and the email link to Dr Andy Gill is a very nice touch. I think that the Game Challenge would produce some very interesting results.

www.charlottestreet.com

Charlotte Street

Overall rating: ★★★

Classification:	Magazine	**Readability:**	★★★
Updating:	Regularly	**Reliability:**	★★★★
Navigation:	★★★	**Speed:**	★★★★

UK

A large and general website aimed at women which divides up into Babies & Family, Look/Feel Great, Work & Money, Love & Marriage, Home & Shopping, Leisure & Freetime and Horoscopes. It comes ultimately from the same stable as Associated Press (publishers of the Daily Mail). The home page of the Babies & Family channel gives a couple of new features such as the Perfect Birth Bag and Kids at Risk from RSI. The Babies & Family channel breaks down into Pregnancy and Babies, Education and Children. There is a home page for each channel which carries up-to-date features, but there are no references to the articles' source which would be useful .

SPECIAL FEATURES

The Pregnancy section breaks down into:

The Facts Everything you need to know about having a baby. Your pregnancy week by week which provides very straightforward information on the development of the baby in the womb.

Pregnancy Possible Problems is an easy guide, providing information by symptom. As well as a week by week Pregnancy Diary by someone called Sarah Ashford.

Ask the experts, has two gynaecologists answering health problems.

The Children section opens with features such as road safety and a new company manufacturing satellite trackers integrated into children's clothes so you can track their movements. This then breaks down into:

Childcare including your rights, what type of childcare, and how to find childcare.

Schoolchildren features articles on the effect of TV, on learning problems, and on the uses of computers in schools.

Preteenagers contains articles on internet guidance, behaviour and self-esteem, peer group pressure.

Teenagers features sex education, living with a teenager and handling a teenage party.

Young Adults covers part-time jobs, dealing with teenage pregnancy, and how to keep your child drug-free.

Problems covers things which cut across the ages for example discipline, sibling rivalry, truancy, poor grades, suspension/expulsion, bullying, lying, criminal activity.

The Education section covers schooling from First School, Home Schooling through to Secondary Schools, Getting Involved, Further Education and Higher Education. Each section is full of advice on how to prepare your child for the next stage, about exams, and about becoming involved, such as becoming a governor.

There are also message boards for eight general areas, ranging from trying for a baby to schooldays (most messages focus on trying for a baby).

Links to other sites: include direct links to numerous advertisers (such as Direct Line, Virgin and Debenhams).

When it comes to parenting, this site really only scores points for its pregnancy and education coverage...overall it's too generalist to be of great value. But it's worth a quick dip and gives a very good overview of what new parents might expect....

www.gingerbread.org.uk

Gingerbread

Overall rating: ★★★			
Classification:	Charity	**Readability:**	★★★
Updating:	Weekly	**Reliability:**	★★★★★
Navigation:	★★★★	**Speed:**	★★★★

UK

This is the website for the UK-based charity for lone parents. It is also a membership organisation (print out and fill in the form and send with £5), although this doesn't prohibit access to the site. Primarily a support and resource organisation for lone parents, complete with a freephone advice line, it also provides a general information service on all sorts of issues regarding lone parenthood and gives information about local groups which operate nationally. Gingerbread's help with children is documented on the site, through a series of networks, the charity has organised 10,000 children of lone parents to meet others in similar situations to reassure each other and to boost confidence.

SPECIAL FEATURES

Calling all Lone Fathers is a new project by Gingerbread to identify and promote the vews and needs of lone fathers, they are looking for single fathers to participate.

Join our journalist register if you are a lone parent keen to tell your story to a journalist for print or for TV, this is an appeal for volunteers to print and fill in the form and send it in.

Virtual Gingerbread is the discussion forum to air views and sympathies on areas relating to child rearing and other problems associated with lone parents.

This is a straightforward website giving good details about the charity, its financing, its advice, and publications on an area of parenting that is growing rapidly.

www.channelhealth.net

Channel Health

Overall rating: ★★★			
Classification:	Organisation	**Readability:**	★★★★★
Updating:	Regularly	**Reliability:**	★★★★
Navigation:	★★★★	**Speed:**	★★★★

UK

A good-looking, UK-based site linked to the satellite television channel of the same name. Due to expand, the site currently blends alternative approaches to health issues with more orthodox health news from sites such as www.health-news.co.uk. Navigation is fairly easy once you've worked out the key to the obscure symbols on the home page. Parents will want to go in via TT (Toddler Taming) or THC (Teen Health), although they may find that their stressed lives lead them to seek out Chill, or even Pleasure Principle (PP) if they've got the energy. Within each section clear buttons on the left-hand side deliver access to topics from a limited but well-chosen list of articles at the bottom of the page (you may need to scroll to find them). Alternatively you can use the Search facility, which has a pull-down menu of keywords, but not all the topics they cover are listed and it would certainly be a shame to miss out on their very useful head lice article!

SPECIAL FEATURES

Toddler Taming is the most promising area for parents, and although focused on younger children and babies it has a wider appeal than the name suggests. Articles are loosely grouped under the headings Bringing Up Baby, Terrible Twos, Growing Up and Baby Doctor.

Health shop lists items such as natural toiletries from the Barefoot doctor to books and tapes, with orders sent via the individual suppliers. The shopping facility is still in development and due to expand.

Other Features

Teen health doesn't deliver as much as it promises: the articles under such headings as Sex'nStuff, Drugs, Chill Pill and Blues Busters are mostly written neither for nor about teenagers specifically. Your Say provides an email opportunity to express views and raise queries, but as these are not posted on the site it's hard to gauge how active this sections is. Could do better...

There is a strong alternative angle to the material on this site, so this needs to be taken into account when considering the information given for subjects such as antibiotics, but overall it takes a well-balanced approach to health matters. There are plans to expand more into the pregnancy/baby/child care area, so it will increasingly become a site of value to parents.

www.parenthoodweb.com

Parenthoodweb

Overall rating: ★★★

Classification:	Information	**Readability:**	★★
Updating:	Regularly	**Reliability:**	★★★★
Navigation:	★★★	**Speed:**	★★★

US

An extensive American site covering subjects as diverse as infertility to teenagers and offering a wealth of information in a variety of forms from a range of experts, including parents themselves. A subsidary of United Advertising Publications, Inc (a United News & Media Company).

Fair – it could do with a more general home page overview outlining its aim and the range of the site, but there is a Topic section which indexes the sites from ADHD (attention deficit hyperactive disorder) to Y2K (year two thousand). Along the top of the screen are buttons to several areas: Home, Shopping, Pregnancy, Names, Recipes, Sleep, Horoscopes, Chat, Boards, Topic (articles under this category link to discussion forums on specific subjects, such as sleep, and also link to other related articles). The whole site is a bit confusing to browse, as well as the subject buttons along the top, there are lists of subjects on the left and various pull-down menus (favourites, pregnancy) scattered around the home page.

SPECIAL FEATURES

Pregnancy section is a large searchable database with articles on almost anything you could think of to do with pregnancy and related subjects. These include foetal development, back pain, ante-natal classes, dad's roles, episiotomy, miscarriage, nutrition, siblings, turning the baby, VBAC (vaginal birth after caesarean), and waterbirth.

Names is a database where you can enter a baby's name and get a quick meaning, as well as lists of the most popular boy's and girl's names (in the USA, in 1997 so of limited interest here except to see how the names differ!). There are also articles about naming your baby.

Surveys visitors are asked to complete optional surveys on a range of subjects, which no doubt provides the parent company with valuable information it can utilise or sell on!

Other features

These include a chat room, children's health tips, shopping (via links), horoscopes, recipes and similar.

Links to other sites include www.SmarterKids.com, www.toysmart.com, BarnesandNoble.com, eToys.com and others. Also to websites for some of the experts whose articles are available, such as www.drpaula.com.

www.parentingproject.org

Parenting Project

Overall rating: ★★★			
Classification:	Information	**Readability:**	★★★★
Updating:	Erratic	**Reliability:**	★★★★
Navigation:	★★★★	**Speed:**	★★★★

US

This is a small site aimed at informing parents, teachers, educators and public officials about focusing on parenting education for teenagers. The programme is designed to address problems such as teen pregnancy, child abuse and overall violence and it provides details of the Baby Think It Over infant simulator programme and results of what students, parents and teachers think of it. The site is generally good for its type, but too limited for general parenting interest, it is easy to find your way around as there are only ten main pages, with interlinks.

SPECIAL FEATURES

Baby Think It Over is a new programme designed to help teenagers understand the commitment and responsibility of parenting. The teenagers are given an 'infant simulator', a computerized 'baby' programmed to cry at random day and night. Like a real infant it deprives the teenagers of sleep, disrupts their social lives and attracts disapproving looks in public. The teenager must feed, change, burp and generally care for the 'baby' and any neglect or abuse is detected by the computer including mishandling that could lead to 'shaken baby syndrome'.

Other features

There are also articles on child abuse and neglect, cycles of violence, teen pregnancy, the need for empathy and non-violent communication, and relationship skills.

Links to other sites are listed under Resources & Links which lead to related, parenting education resources.

This is a US-based site promoting parenting education and the teaching of parenting skills in primary and secondary schools. It has a well laid out mission-vision-implementation plan designed to promote the learning of parenting skills and to create caring classroom environments. It is attempting to prepare tomorrow's parents today by bringing these topics into the North American teaching curriculum. The site is designed to advertise the courses and training resources available in the States.

www.postiveparenting.com

Positive Parenting On-Line

Overall rating: ★★★

Classification:	Personal	**Readability:**	★★★
Updating:	Not good	**Reliability:**	★★★★
Navigation:	★★★★	**Speed:**	★★★

US

This site was developed and is maintained by parenthood educator Deborah Critzer. Based in California, she provides details of local classes, workshops, training programmes, and similar, which are only relevant to those in the vicinity. The extent and content of the material is focused on positive parenting from birth to adolescence. There is good information about six specific professional organisations and resources, carefully chosen to reflect the aims and approach of the site. Extensive message boards are also available via a direct link to www.parentsplace.com.

It is easy to navigate with a page index that is clearly accessible and the pages are interlinked. The headings include What's New, Newsletter, Feature Articles, Organisations, Expert Index, Links, and so on. However, in March 2000, the What's New was still on Fall 1999 – not so new!

SPECIAL FEATURES

Expert index links to parenting resources in 20 US states, plus four parenting resources in Australia.

Positive Parenting is a newsletter which you have to subscribe to. The contents listing of each issue is available from the site via the Bookstore so you can buy back issues if you want to.

Feature Tips and Articles about positive parenting issues, mainly regarding children's difficult behaviour and punishments.

Positive Parenting Bookstore has a selection of books, tapes and videos to sell on carefully chosen related topics.

There is an actual **Links** page, listing 62 related sites – from The National Parenting Centre to Yahooligans, and the Discovery Channel School to Water Birth Information. There is also a direct link to the US-based International Network for Children and Families, accessible at www.redirectingbehavior.com - the parent organisation for the site.

Although this site is quite American in feel, there are some good parenting techniques and tactics covered, usually in the form of a personal anecdote. It is also far less commercial than many sites, being free from copious advertising.

www.thelaboroflove.com

The Labor of Love

Overall rating: ★★★

Classification:	Magazine	**Readability:**	★★★
Updating:	Monthly	**Reliability:**	★★★
Navigation:	★★	**Speed:**	★★★

US

A US-based, magazine-style site with a good range of informative articles from parenting 'experts', including people such as UK homeopath Miranda Castro. The section headings range from Pregnancy and Childbirth to Family Time, via Breastfeeding (The Nursing Nook), to Food for Thought (which is nothing about nutrition). However, each category contains several articles which need a lot of scrolling down. Anyone can send in an article and hope to have it published which makes for a variety of stories, some are very schmaltzy!

SPECIAL FEATURES

New Arrivals is online birth announcements. You can add your own announcement or view other people's, and press the button next to theirs to send a congratulations message. I'm not sure how much I'd want a message from someone I didn't know, and some of the current announcements are tragic - announcing births and deaths simultaneously.

News headlines gives access to world news via ParentMail.com and is a useful antidote to some of this site's content.

Journals provided by contributors is extensive coverage of individual stories ranging from those who are trying to conceive (currently 28 'journalers' recording journals) to pregnancy stories. This might be of interest to those going through similar experiences. Lots of birth stories have been posted (currently 480!).

The Family Room An online pregnancy and parenting magazine with articles and essays on a range of subjects under the categories of humour, essays, pregnancy, childcare and health. These articles are posted up one after another so you have to scroll down a long way and you would be hard pushed to keep reading to the end.

Collection of Freebies Clicking on this opens up a new browser so you can easily find your way back to the home page. At the time of review it was running four links to freebies and to two magazines offering a first issue free.

Links exist to ParentMail.com and a number of commercial sites, such as BabyUniverse.com and amazon.com and babiesonline.com for free birth announcements.

This is a whimsical site which UK visitors might find rather American in its sentimentality (the online birth announcements and the rather extraordinary journals each being a case in point). This is very much a 'sharing/caring' website.

www.everywoman.co.uk

Everywoman

Overall rating: ★★★

Classification:	Magazine	**Readability:**	★★★
Updating:	Regularly	**Reliability:**	★★★★
Navigation:	★★★	**Speed:**	★★★

UK

UK-based site set up by Maxine Benson and Karen Gill. The parenting aspect of the site is only part of the story -- finance, law, money, travel, technology, the garden and natural remedies, it's just about all there! But the actual content in each area is very limited. The homepage has an easy index, necessary for such a vast site, which directs you straight to the Family Channel. This is then divided into Pregnancy & Maternity, Children, Parenting, Relationships and the Classroom.

SPECIAL FEATURES

Ask the expert Currently only one, Jill Curtis, psychoanalytic psychotherapist who has her own personal website (www.family2000.org.uk – see p19).

Bulletin board Always fascinating, and for specific queries a useful way to share information.

Classroom Weekly worksheets and a direct link to www.learningco.com, plus 'ask the tutor' option (Jill Curtis).

Library option gives a range of specific articles, although some of these are limited. Getting ready for school, for example, is actually a review for a Getting Ready for School video and details of how to buy it, although that is useful in itself. Useful Tips when Pregnant only gives details of caring for your back. So perhaps some of these are a missed opportunity for information.

Infobank has a search facility for specific help groups and organisations – although when 'cleft palate' and 'association for post-natal illness' were entered it returned four pages of organisations, and neither of these two were listed.

Links to other sites Bookshop option links to amazon.co.uk but apart from the ubiquitous Amazon, there are links to five kids-oriented sites and one to a baby name site. The site also links to selected articles on the Guardian's news unlimited site.

There is definitely room for some development on the content of the site's categories.

www.parentlineplus.org.uk

Parentline

Overall rating: ★★

Classification:	Charity	**Readability:**	★★
Updating:	regularly	**Reliability:**	★★★★
Navigation:	★★	**Speed:**	★★

UK

This is primarily an information site linked to the freephone Parentline help number. Parentline Plus was formed by the merger between Parentline and the National Stepfamily Association.

This website is ripe for development. It is linking to parent network in Spring 2000, a site currently under construction.

Chapter 2

Pregnancy and Childbirth

Numerous organisations and charities exist to promote information about pregnancy and childbirth, often providing quite specific agendas but also very good and informative websites. These tend to provide information supplementary to what you might receive from your own doctor or midwife, and as a result are often perceived as slightly alternative in nature. Whether or not this is your individual bag, there is a range of excellent information that is well worth a look, and access to more in-depth material than might be otherwise available to you.

Pregnancy Issues

There is much to be done in preparation for the birth of a baby, ranging from consideration of what sort of birth to opt for, plus finding out details of National Childbirth Trust classes, or even dealing with the sad event of a miscarriage which affects around 1 in 4 couples. Fortunately there are numberous organisations and contacts available to help and these are becoming increasingly accessible via the internet.

www.homebirth.org.uk

Angela Horn

Overall rating: ★★★★★

Classification:	Personal	**Readability:**	★★★
Updating:	Weekly	**Reliability:**	★★★★
Navigation:	★★★	**Speed:**	★★★★

UK

This is an excellent, small, very specific, non-commercial site for parents considering the home birth option, owned and maintained by Angela Horn (a research academic) as a public service. The inspiration for the site was her own good home birth experience.

SPECIAL FEATURES

Home Birth Stories some very positive but others less so.

Contact us Personal email to Angela Horn

Other features
An interesting list of summarised research papers. Articles are posted up fairly regularly on topics such as transfers to hospital from home, since November 1999.

Links to sites such as the Independent Midwives, Association for Improvement in the Maternity Services, and the British Medical Journal editorial.

The site isn't evangelical, but provides good, peer-reviewed research-based support on the subject, lists local groups, and links to other supportive networks.

www.activebirthcentre.com The Active Birth Centre			
Overall rating: ★★★★			
Classification:	Organisation	**Readability:**	★★★★
Updating:	Regularly	**Reliability:**	★★★★
Navigation:	★★★★	**Speed:**	★★★★
UK			

This UK-site outlines the best of the active birth approach, providing additional support via training days (London-based). There are also links to independent midwives and active birth teachers.

SPECIAL FEATURES

Education This section is very informative, giving the aims of the organisation to educate, empower and inspire women to have confidence in their ability to give birth. There is a detailed list of ante-natal and post-natal programmes and workshops on subjects such as yoga, breastfeeding, water births, vaccination issues, homeopathy, baby massage and even belly dancing (which can ease the pain of labour!) There is also contact information for certified active birth teachers.

Birth Pools is a on-line catalogue of birthing pools and accessories for hire, with prices and delivery details as well as general information

ABC News is regular bulletin featuring relevant news items such the health hazards warning in aromatherapy oils.

Other Features

Online shop and mail order catalogue with extensive range of books on natural birth and yoga, plus aromatherapy products, nursing bras, and more. There is also a newsletter but his hadn't been updated for three months.

There are links to related sites such as www.homebirth.org.uk and www.birthcentre.com.

A well-focused, informative site with a clear home page.

www.aims.org.uk

Association for Improvements in the Maternity Services

Overall rating: ★★★

Classification:	Organisation	**Readability:**	★★★★
Updating:	Regularly	**Reliability:**	★★★★★
Navigation:	★★★	**Speed:**	★★★★

UK

AIMS stands for the Association for Improvements in the Maternity Services and the website serves mainly as an introduction to the membership organisation. AIMS was originally set up by Beverly Beech, a tireless campaigner for improvements in maternity services and it seeks to provide research, information and support to parents and professionals in an effort to improve maternity services.

SPECIAL FEATURES

Research feature gives access to selected articles from AIMS' journal.

Publications AIMS publications available to order are listed, complete with order form.

Contact us You can contact Beverly Beech and others by phone or email.

Other Features

News gives details of forthcoming AIMS activities (such as conferences for professionals and parents alike).

Links Excellent links to relevant childbirth, midwifery, and general health and medical sites.

This is a research-based, straightforward site and is designed to link visitors to the parent organisation.

www.apni.org

The Association for Post-Natal Illness

Overall rating: ★★★

Classification:	Charity	**Readability:**	★★★★
Updating:	None	**Reliability:**	★★★★★
Navigation:	★★★★	**Speed:**	★★★

UK

Apni is a small, focused site from the Association for Post-Natal Illness, which affects between 70,000 and 100,000 women a year. Unfortunately due to lack of funding this site has become static and its future is uncertain.

SPECIAL FEATURES

Our Function offers information specifically about post-natal illness in general. The registered charity aims to offer support to sufferers, increase public awareness and to encourage research.

Newsletter but the last one posted at the time of review was five months out of date.

Primarily a support organisation serving a vital function, the site does little more than provide some basic information and, most importantly, a Helpline phone number and personal email addresses at the Association.

www.sheilakitzinger.com

Sheila Kitzinger

Overall rating: ★★★

Classification:	Personal	**Readability:**	★★★★
Updating:	regularly	**Reliability:**	★★★★
Navigation:	★★★★	**Speed:**	★★★

UK

The personal website of Sheila Kitzinger, the guru of pregnancy and childbirth, social anthropologist, midwifery lecturer and writer. This is an non-commercial site focusing on Sheila Kitzinger's campaigning work, and it includes access to her publications via amazon.co.uk. Serves as an introduction to the site-owner's work and there are also articles by guest columnists, changed every 'few months'. The site is easy to navigate as all the site content icons appear at the bottom of each page and it is easy to find your way back to the home page.

SPECIAL FEATURES

Sheila's Work and what people say about it gives reviews of recently published articles by Sheila Kitzinger and details of her books, both published and forthcoming.

Birth images (slow to download) is a selection of illustrations and poetry by Sheila Kitzinger.

Birth action addresses the rising Caesarean rates in the UK, and looks at various prosecutions of midwives and offers support for them.

Mothers and babies in prison. Sheila is campaigning to provide a nationwide network of support through the use of doulas (a project begun in Holloway prison), but it is in the early planning stages.

Guest column of articles by other writers, changed every few months but currently featuring Polly Kitzinger, Bianca Lapori, Marcia May and Mary Newburn.

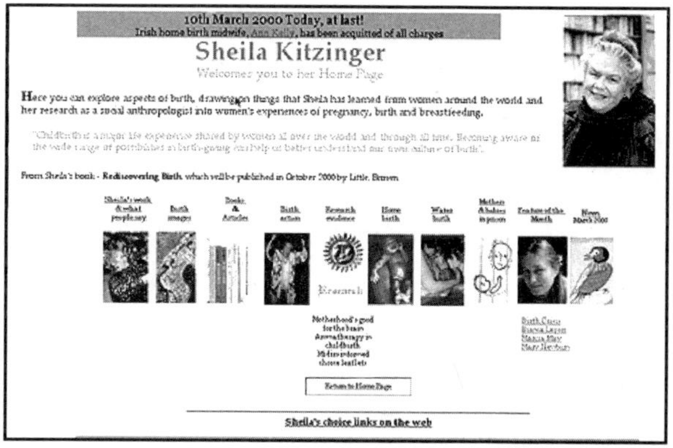

Other Features include information on home births and water births.

Links to the NCT, midirs (midwives information and resource service), British Medical Journal, Mothering (a US-based natural family magazine), and to the US-based Lamaze International.

A wonderful site!

www.the-ma.org.uk

The Miscarriage Association

Overall rating: ★★★

Classification:	Charity	**Readability:**	★★★★
Updating:	Erratic	**Reliability:**	★★★★
Navigation:	★★★★	**Speed:**	★★★

UK

Site for the Miscarriage Association, a charity that provides reasonably up-to-date information on this difficult topic as well as support to women who have miscarried their babies. It is a very good support website for all those women who miscarry and find they have no-one to talk to.

The information section gives an overview of the charity and explains that it gathers information about courses and treatments and promotes good hospital practice. There is a network of over 200 volunteer support contacts and 50 groups throughout the UK.

It is an active site (33,000 hits since May 1999) for a non-commercial charity but when reviewed the site hadn't been updated for a couple of months. There is information on how you can provide help through sponsorship.

SPECIAL FEATURES

Guestbook Features personal stories written by women who have experienced the sadness of miscarriage.

Suggested reading is a list of relevant publications each with a click through to amazon.co.uk to buy the book online.

Links Excellent, well-organised links categorised by Newsgroups, Information, Memorial, Support, and Other. These link to sites ranging from simple support, to information held in larger sites, as well as to very specific medical information.

Other Features includes information on how to become a volunteer or a fund raiser.

This site is recommended to anyone seeking support after a miscarriage.

www.nct-online.org The National Childbirth Trust			
Overall rating: ★★			
Classification:	Charity	**Readability:**	★★★★
Updating:	Regularly	**Reliability:**	★★★★
Navigation:	★★★	**Speed:**	★★
UK			

The NCT is the main antenatal and childbirth charity in the UK and it is primarily a membership organisation. This site serves as an introduction to the NCT and is designed to solicit membership. Because of this there is limited direct information given on the subject other than a sample of articles from its publication New Generation.

SPECIAL FEATURES

Recent Updates Immediate NCT responses to news items. For example, a new report on alcohol in pregnancy released in January 2000 received an NCT comment dated the same day. There was also an article on having a baby when you're over 35 and the associated risks of having a miscarriage, or of being aware of the likelihood of having a baby with Downs Syndrome. There is advice on ante-natal classes and on breastfeeding, both of which link through to the contact the NCT page.

Membership Information is given about what NCT antenatal classes cover, but no direct contact information. Those interested are referred to the head office via mail or telephone, but no email contact is currently available.

Special offer of a free NCT authorised book when joining the NCT, offer open until September 2000. The membership form is not user-friendly, with lots of pages to fill in before being asked to print it out and send it in with payment.

Links There is a direct link to the NCT Maternity sales website, to NCT publishing, and to other relevant sites such as La Leche League, Baby Milk Action and TAMBA (Twins and Multiple Births Association).

A rather cumbersome site to navigate, aimed at promoting the charity with not very much detailed information. Worth a visit though if you are interested in joining the NCT.

Pregnancy Products

An inevitable consequence of being pregnant is the need to clothe an ever - increasing girth. The net has provided a home for numerous specialist outlets to extend their market with online ordering.

In addition, the net is home to one of the most useful pregnancy product sites run by midwife Zita West, complete with extensive back - up information and support about all aspects of pregnancy.

www.zitawest.com

Zita West Pregnancy Products (FKA: The Pregnancy Shop)

Overall rating: ★★★★★

Classification:	Personal	**Readability:**	★★★★
Updating:	Regularly	**Reliability:**	★★★★★
Navigation:	★★★★★	**Speed:**	★★★

UK

This is primarily a selling site, wholly owned and managed by practising midwife and acupuncturist, Zita West. It is a good example of a personal website, being friendly, accessible, and informative.

SPECIAL FEATURES

Complementary Medicine gives advice about what you can and cannot take in pregnancy.

Shopping Centre Direct order for a range of pre-conception, antenatal and postnatal products, primarily for mothers.

Contact us opportunity for any queries via email, telephone or post.

Other Features

Extensive information on pre-conception health, the trimesters of pregnancy, nutrition and complementary medicine, complete with extensive information from expert practitioners.

This is an excellent small site for easily accessible information on pregnancy in general.

www.jojomamanbebe.co.uk

Jojo Maman Bebe

Overall rating: ★★★★

Classification:	E-commerce	**Readability:**	★★★★
Updating:	Regularly	**Reliability:**	★★★★
Navigation:	★★★★	**Speed:**	★★★

UK

This is a site for online shopping from this diverse mail-order shop, divided up by collections. there is also a **Product Search** throughout the on-line catalogue. You can click on **Your Order** at any point to check how your order is building and how much money you are spending.

The **Help** section gives advice on sizing (use your pre-preganant size unless your bust has increased by more than 3 inches), how to measure yourself for a nursing bra, how the babies and children's sizes work (by age, height and weight as well as for socks, shoes and hat sizes). The customer service and delivery details can also be found under the Help section.

SPECIAL FEATURES

Maternity Collection gives a great selection of clothes for the pregnant woman of today. You click on each thumbnail photo to enlarge the selected item and a list of the other items in that category also appears and again, you click on the name to produce a photograph. The categories in this section are currently businesswear, summer eveningwear, mix and match basics, smart casual, weekend wear, summer casuals, holiday essentials, nighwear, underwear and nursing tops.

Baby and Kids Collections is a range of nicely designed clothes ranging in size from 3 months to 5 years, categorised by 'collection' including a basics directory, hot pinks, nautical, safari, swimtime, sleepsuits and rompers, pyjamas, accessories (socks, tights, hats) and outerwear.

Practical Products contains a wide selection of useful baby equipment nder the headings of preparing for a new baby, breats and bottle feeding, sleep training (and nursery decoration), changing bags and baby carriers, potty training and nappy changing , baby bathtime, weaning and feeding, car safety and accessories, holiday and travel.

Gift and toys provides a range suitable for presents such as birth anouncement cards, christening and baby gifts, newborn and baby toys, toddler toys and big kids (3-5 years).

Clearance Sale is the reduced price sale area for both the maternity and the kids clothes.

Other Features

These include ordering a free catalogue via mail, recommend a friend and get a £5 gift voucher, and secure online ordering of anything from the collection.

This is a great one-stop service with a very nicely designed range of clothes, as well as presents.

www.bloomingmarvellous.co.uk			
Blooming Marvellous Ltd			
Overall rating: ★★★			
Classification:	E-commerce	**Readability:**	★★★★
Updating:	Regularly	**Reliability:**	★★★★
Navigation:	★★★★	**Speed:**	★★★
UK			

This is the website for the popular mail order pregnancy and baby catalogue. It has a straightforward, basic supply of pregnancy and new baby clothes, plus a good range of nursery items from E-Z bathers, protect and play mats, baby head supports, handbags highchairs, and so on.

You can browse the site and review the collection. The shopping is easy to use with straightforward 'add to bag' or 'go to checkout' buttons next to each item. The online ordering service takes all major credit cards and offers a one hundred per cent secure ordering service. There is also a free catalogue ordering service which you can send to friends – and it asks for comments.

SPECIAL FEATURES

Help is a very good section for answering order queries (includes FAQs and secure ordering/payment details plus a phone number).

Fun and games section (in case you get bored with ordering baby clothes!). You can play computer games, calculate your due date, and send E-cards to other expectant or newly delivered friends.

Fast shop is a page where you can order directly from the catalogue by filling in an online form (if you have the catalogue in front of you and are an existing customer) instead of browsing the website and collecting up orders in the shopping basket. This certainly saves you online time.

Other Features

It is worth noting the **Sale!** page where you can pick up a bargain. Details are also given of the Blooming Marvellous shops nationwide and of their **Top Ten Nursery Products.**

Links appear under subject category. For example the Baby Names section is a collection of links to babynames.com, babyzone.com and Amazon.com.

www.formes.com
Formes

Overall rating: ★★★

Classification:	E-commerce	**Readability:**	★
Updating:	Occasionally	**Reliability:**	★★
Navigation:	★	**Speed:**	★★

UK

An online service for the French maternity fashion boutique, providing details of the shops worldwide available in either English or French language.

You can choose to view the site either as an HTML version or as an animated version. (Shockwave is required but available to download for free.)

The site is well-designed, and has pop-up frames to show you how the clothes work to fit your increasing girth as pregnancy progresses. The graphics are good and clear.

The downside is that you cannot order online. You need to either order a printed catalogue to be sent to you, or you can print out an order form and fax or mail it. Telephone and fax numbers are available for help. Although this is a French company, the clothes are warehoused and sent from the UK so the £3 post and packing charge is comparable to other UK mail-order clothes companies.

You need perseverance to succeed with this one; although the design looks good, it is not very user-friendly and it's difficult to work out how to actually buy something!

Chapter 3

Babies

Early parenthood can be an especially daunting time, with so much to learn of a practical nature while wrestling with the inevitable emotional seesaws. Finding out as much as possible about nappy options for example, or accessing information at 3 a.m. about what is a 'normal' sleep pattern or how to take a temperature, can become almost an obsession during the early months as parents try to get to grips with this momentous life change. Most sites also include information about pregnancy and birth, the assumption being that you will probably start finding out about newborn and infant care before giving birth. There is also access to online product ordering, in some cases, which reflects the difference between life before and after giving birth - getting to the shops suddenly becomes an herculean task, involving many more bits and pieces than just your credit card!

www.babyparenting.about.com

About.com

Overall rating: ★★★★★

Classification:	Magazine	**Readability:**	★★★
Updating:	Frequently	**Reliability:**	★★★
Navigation:	★★★	**Speed:**	★★

US

This American website is generally unpatronising and straightforward with an excellent selection of resources. The site is run by a designated 'guide', Lynn M Johnson, who has completed college courses in psychology, human development, child development, communications and sociology, she also has three children. The information is detailed and quite clinical, with references and links to academic publications, but it also includes more personal and anecdotal additions. For example, updates on vaccines includes a link to the AAP (American Academy of Pediatrics) but also includes an information exchange between interested parents on the Forum. There is also a detailed search facility to find subjects within the site. For example, a search for 'homeopathy' listed 246 related documents. There is also the facility to share the site with a friend.

SPECIAL FEATURES

Member page Joining this website gives you a member page, with your own URL and a listing in their member directory – an ideal way 'to tell the world about yourself and your interests...'.

ShopCenter which links to US online shopping.

Other features

As a part of About.com, this website is directly linked to those commerical parties who feature as partners to About.com. In addition, as part of a network of sites led by expert guides, once into babyparenting.about.com you are linked to a massive array of around 650 other informative sites covering a multitude of topics. The site also lists direct links to 16 allied parenting sites such as Fatherhood, Single Parents, Parenting of Adolescents, and so on.

The site has a massive array of informative links to subjects as diverse as brain research and potty training. The news headlines do tend to be US-focused (with Burger King recalling 25 million promotional Pokemon Balls, for example) but it does have good resources and a large database of information.

www.babycenter.com

Baby Center

Overall rating: ★★★★

Classification:	Magazine	**Readability:**	★★
Updating:	Daily	**Reliability:**	★★★
Navigation:	★★	**Speed:**	★★★★

US

This is a wholly owned subsidiary of eToys.com. It is a US-based site founded in 1997. Although they claim to be the only site who uses a team of medical experts to ensure the reliability of their advice, this is no longer true as many other sites now do the same. The site is not terribly easy to navigate and requires a lot of to-ing and fro-ing to gain access to some parts such as the bulletin board. However, the expert advice is excellent for a wide range of baby features and there is a regular chat auditorium with an expert (for example, a chat with Dr Jodi Mindell, child psychologist, about sleep proplems in babies). The UK based version (babycenter.co.uk is coming soon)

SPECIAL FEATURES

Stage-by-stage information keying in your baby's age gives you access to personalised, age-related information. However, to find the heading 'Discipline' after keying in 'four months', complete with a feature on temper tantrums in babies, and then to be linked to a feature stating that 94 per cent of parents use corporal punishment with their toddlers was a bit alarming. (Although this was then linked to two articles by eminent psychologists, both of whom oppose smacking.)

Babystore is a shopping area with a membership facility offering special bargains but only accessible via US at present.

Free stuff register here for e-mail information about your baby's development, access to free samples, special offers etc.

Today's features new articles by experts on a range of subjects from conception to solid foods to baby name polls.

Bulletin board where parents can share ideas and tips.

Links Some articles are actually sponsored by a commercial manufacturer, and clearly marked as such. For example, Johnson & Johnson sponsor a baby massage feature with a direct link to a product-promoting site (although with very good information).

The site covers preconception to toddler, and because you can personalise it to your own stage of pregnancy or to the age of your children it is excellent for accessing what you want to know now and what may be relevant over the next few months.No doubt when the site becomes UK-specific it will be of greater value to parents.

www.babyworld.co.uk Babyworld			
Overall rating: ★★★★			
Classification:	Magazine	**Readability:**	★★★★★
Updating:	Weekly	**Reliability:**	★★★★★
Navigation:	★★★★★	**Speed:**	★★★★
UK			

Babyworld was started by Radcliffe Medical Press, an authoritative Oxford-based medical publisher, but it is now published as a subsidiary of Freeserve. It is produced very much as an interactive magazine aimed at pregnant and new mothers. Its editor-in-chief, Anita Bevan, is a veteran of this area of magazine publishing and it shows. The site is straightforward with clear listings and logical sequencing although the large amount of banner advertising can be irritating.

SPECIAL FEATURES

News & features the benefit of this section is that additional information is given to recent news stories. For example, on a news item about parental leave, information was included to provide back-up together with links to other areas of interest within the site.

Your experiences leads to a discussion forum with other members providing access to ideas and information and for meeting other members

Ask our experts A team of 'experts' including a doctor and a midwife. Individual and personal questions can be asked of these, and the replies are available to all. The extent of information given in the replies is excellent, comprehensive and unpatronising. This makes the site an excellent source of information to all new parents as, although the answers are question-specific, lots of the questions cover common topics and concerns. Where appropriate, links are given to other sites or sources of helpful information.

Don't Miss gives membership joining details, a competition and an opportunity to meet the team behind the website.

Products & Shopping is for product testing and choosing as well as shopping featuring over 500 new product lines

Member benefits gives access to some member-only areas plus offers and competitions, membership is free upon registration.

Other features

Essential information on trying for a baby, on pregnancy and birth, on being new parents, on childcare and on health is given in other sections and ones which one would certainly return to as your child grows.

Links there are extensive links to advertisers and, where applicable, their websites. These range from Huggies nappies, to Johnson & Johnson, Urchin kids mail order, Children's Health Co., and Circle: The Women's Channel.

This website is based on the traditional magazine format with good clear information on every aspect of birth and childcare and development. I would recommend a visit by a mother with young babies at home who wants up to date readable advice on these subjects.

www.babydirectory.com

The Baby Directory

Overall rating: ★★★

Classification:	Information	**Readability:**	★★★★
Updating:	Monthly	**Reliability:**	★★★★
Navigation:	★★★★	**Speed:**	★★★★

UK

This site is an information-led, independently owned and uncommercial website, linked to the London Baby Directory (which is also franchised in five other UK areas). It has parent-friendly text, both non-patronising and clear with easy, one-step access to the main sites from the home page, clearly listed and itemised.

SPECIAL FEATURES

Doctor's Surgery Medical advice provided by a literate doctor, but it's clear about when to contact your own GP. There is also an online service for raising specific medical queries.

Breastfeeding counsellors available via email or directly through telephone contact. This shows a real commitment to parents!

Book shop Some book reviews featuring those thought to be of intrinsic interest and value, and include both children's and parenting titles. So you will find Harry Potter, but not Noddy. Although not extensive as yet, this section is one that will probably expand as more books are reviewed. There is a direct link to amazon.co.uk to buy books.

Features on different parenting topics (such as finding childcare, walking to school and music for kids) are of general and specific interest and give a magazine-y feel to this website's content.

Holidays in the UK are advertised with a searchable location map, currently thin on choice but could be very useful when more information is available.

Other features

Buy your local Baby Directory with a location map showing what areas the directory currently covers. Nanny Agency section provides links to the London-based Childminders babysitting agency and The London Nanny Company to which you can register online. There is also a 'gift shop' section for online sales which is geared mainly to a few selected products, but with a secure credit card payment service.

Link to kidskiosk.com, which is a useful and active forum for buying and selling second-hand children's clothes and equipment. Other links include the London-based Birth Unit at the Hospital for St John and St Elizabeth, to Childminders and The London Nanny Company. All the links have obvious and easy links back to The Baby Directory

Although quite limited in scope compared to mega-sites such as Babyworld.co this website is due for continued development and has an integrity which makes it friendly and accessible.

www.webbaby.co.uk

WebBaby

Overall rating: ★★★

Classification:	Magazine	**Readability:**	★★★
Updating:	Regularly	**Reliability:**	★★★
Navigation:	★★★	**Speed:**	★★

UK

This is a UK site designed to provide UK parents with the sort of babycare and pregnancy information currently freely available in the US. It was co-founded by Kirsty Oliver, on maternity leave from Price Waterhouse, and Isaac Davies from Goldman Sachs in October 1999. This site reflects the sort of information modern, working mothers expect. The website is clearly laid out with colour-coded sections to remind you of which section you are in, however it was slow to download – perhaps because it has lots of visitors.There is a website search facility which links directly to any entry, avoiding the need to trawl through sections, plus links to related information and articles.

SPECIAL FEATURES

WebBaby Directory is a fairly comprehensive directory (divided into categories) of organisations and charities which may be of interest/help to parents. There are, however, some oddities (for example, the Advisory Centre for Education is listed under the Illness and Disability category).

Baby boutique with direct ordering facility, although product lines are limited. For example, under Books only one title is listed on 'morning sickness' – which presupposes you may not get any further!

Dr Web's clinic has a directory of symptoms and remedies of childhood illnesses as well as common pregnancy complaints. The site advertises an on-line clinic session but due to technical difficulties this was temporarily suspended although email contact with specialists is possible.

Pregnancy Pack requires you to to register giving details of your due dates etc. WebBaby will then email you with relevant information about employment issues at the correct date. However some people may be reticent about filling in details of their employers in order that WebBaby writes to them about your rights...

Interactive tools allows you to calculate, for example, your risk by maternal age of having a baby with chromosomal abnormality. There is also a Community Chat room, message board, gossip section (although no gossip had been recorded for two weeks!).

Other features

Information about preconception, pregnancy, baby and also covering toddler years for either those parents with enough foresight to think ahead or those with older children. For example, there is good information about finding nursery and infant schools.

Links None, although one obvious place would be to link to those organisations listed in the WebBaby Directory which have sites. For example, the Meningitis Trust has an excellent website for worried parents!

Overall the quality of information is very good and to the point, with an absence of extraneous articles. There is little advertising but a membership scheme which requires logging-in complete with email address. Unfortunately there is no guest log-in system to enable prospective members to check out the facility.

www.greenbabyco.com

Green Baby Co

Overall rating: ★★

Classification:	E-commerce	**Readability:**	★★★★
Updating:	6 monthly	**Reliability:**	★
Navigation:	★★★	**Speed:**	★★★

UK

This is a site set up in 1999 by the UK-based Green Baby Co. who have a shop in North London. The site is still in development although not much seems to have progressed since October 1999. It is a useful site for parents who want to access reusable nappies and other environmentally friendly products although it does not as yet provide on-line ordering, you can either order by phone or print out the order form and fax it through. The full catalogue is available on site.

Skincare ingredients in Greenbaby products are all listed and explained and environmentally friendly.

This site could be very good if more development is done.

Chapter 4

Health

The health of our babies and children can seem an unceasing preoccupation for parents, and especially for mothers, the traditional custodians of family health. While the family practitioner is our primary resource, so often information helps us to decide whether or not it's useful to see the doctor. In the absence of greater experience, there have been times when we have all agonised about whether or not to call the doctor. And then there are the times when a diagnosis has been made, and further information is both valuable and reassuring, whether it's glue ear or diabetes. One recent innovative use of the internet is that made by the many specialist charities and organisations whose aim it is to support and inform a wider audience, often when a diagnosis has been made. In many cases the website is just the beginning of access to a wider range of material, and a help line.

www.lovelife.hea.org.uk Health Education Authority			
Overall rating: ★★★★★			
Classification:	Government	**Readability:**	★★★
Updating:	Regularly	**Reliability:**	★★★★★
Navigation:	★★★★	**Speed:**	★★★★
UK			

Lovelife is the Health Education Authority's Sexual Health Website. It is designed for young adults (with its very groovy graphics), but also for parents who would like their young adult offspring to access good, up-to-date information about sexual health and related matters without having to take them through it themselves! Click in the Lovelife circle to enter the site.

SPECIAL FEATURES

Get it on! animated graphics showing how to use a condom.

Advice is a comprehensive section on HIV, AIDS, genital herpes, and other sexually transmitted diseases.

Check up! provides details of your nearest sexual health clinic, plus an outline of what such a visit would entail. My Visit uses graphics to show what happens when you visit the clinic (friendly receptionist!) and that you could fill in your details on a card using your first name only.

My Nearest Clinic gives a map of the UK. You click on your area (such as London) to get a list of all the clinics in the area.

PlaySafe is a game (requires Flash4 plug-in, available to download free). If you click on the 'play the game' button it takes you straight into it but seemingly without any instructions.

Clem and Lydia is a video (you need RealPlayer but this can be downloaded) designed to raise awareness of sexually transmitted diseases and the prevention of spreading these by wearing condoms.

Other features

Extras! is a fun section where you can send a suitably salacious e-card to a friend or download a Lovelife screen saver! Or take a look at Lovechat where, today, two experts and one celebrity answered questions live online. The age range of those asking was approximately 14-25.

There are links to a good range of related health subjects -- for example, to Avert, the national aids charity and to Virgin Health.

Look here for advice on everything from sexually transmitted diseases to emergency contraception.

www.surgerydoor.co.uk Surgery Door			
Overall rating: ★★★★★			
Classification:	Informative	**Readability:**	★★★★
Updating:	daily	**Reliability:**	★★★★★
Navigation:	★★★★	**Speed:**	★★★★
UK			

The site acts as an online health service. It is run by Intouch, suppliers of touchscreen health information kiosks to the NHS, and features access via email to Dr Mark Porter, the well-known GP and BBC tele-doctor.

SPECIAL FEATURES

Search facility by word or phrase ('sprain' returned 52 articles).

Medical leads to an extensive range of health features, including a good Emergencies section in collaboration with the Red Cross – recommended reading before these things occur There is also a useful Dictionary.

Doors on the home page offer direct access to areas of particular interest – New Parents, Teenagers, Students and Travellers.

Healthy Living leads to options such as New Parents which covers pregnancy and birth, then covers children aged 0-5 years.

Teenagers have a great section, with information on immunisations, alcohol, drugs, benefits plus a hit list of teenage-type afflictions such as acne, glandular fever, anxiety and drug dependence.

Links to other sites: Dr Porter lists ten sites which he personally recommends. These range from medical information sites such as the Health Education Authority's pages for immunisations, to support charities. Also, each area of particular interest lists helpful websites. There is a direct link to Pharmacy 2, the UK's first online mail order pharmacy.

This is a great site, there are news stories, easy-to-find information and access to direct sale health items (such as Videos for Patients, Condomania, and the Fresh Food Company). For parents, there is information ranging from newborns to teenagers and students, plus a source of enquiry about a multitude of health problems.

www.aap.org

American Academy of Paediatrics

Overall rating: ★★★★

Classification:	Information	**Readability:**	★★★★
Updating:	Regularly	**Reliability:**	★★★★★
Navigation:	★★★★	**Speed:**	★★★★

US

A US-based website for the American Academy of Pediatrics, in their own words 'committed to the attainment of optimal physical, mental and social health and well-being for all infants, children, adolescents, and young adults'.

SPECIAL FEATURES

You and Your Family covers a wide range of information for parents and includes **Child Health Month** (currently focusing on substance abuse) and aimed primarily at parents of teens, with good information on alcohol abuse and underage drinking.

Publications is an excellent resource for the AAP's public education brochures and books. Brochures include those on sleep problems, care of the uncircumcised penis, smoking for teens, and developmental milestones.

Other features

Access to the AAP's press releases and links to the National Institute of Child Health and Human Development (www.nichd.nih.gov), another good US site. There are also links to departments within the AAP which can be useful for information.

This is a good resource for parents who want access to parent-friendly, up-to-date, research-based information from an authoritative and reliable source.

www.asthma.org.uk

National Asthma Campaign

Overall rating: ★★★★

Classification:	Charity	**Readability:**	★★★★
Updating:	Monthly	**Reliability:**	★★★★★
Navigation:	★★★★	**Speed:**	★★★★

UK

The website for the National Asthma Campaign, the UK-based charity for people with asthma.

SPECIAL FEATURES

What is Asthma? aims to answer most of the commonly asked questions about asthma.

Children's section gives the opportunity to join the Junior Asthma Club with its membership magazine and pen pals.

Other features

Details of academic research, including access to the 'latest news' concerning asthma (from synthetic pillows to research with expectant mums), plus archive news features.

There are also details of the asthma Helpline, open weekdays from 9 am to 7 pm.

The site is quite comprehensive in its information, but this is limited to the main aspects of the charity's work.

www.bda-findadentist.org.uk

British Dental Association

Overall rating: ★★★★

Classification:	Informative	**Readability:**	★★★
Updating:	weekly	**Reliability:**	★★★★
Navigation:	★★★★	**Speed:**	★★★★

UK

This is a service provided by the British Dental Association, the national body for UK dentists, and is designed primarily just to help you find a local BDA member dentist. Each dentist has provided contact details, information about services provided, areas of special clinical interest and facilities (for example, wheelchair access and car parking).

SPECIAL FEATURES

More About Find-A-Dentist gives information about the service such as whether dentists are NHS or private and that each one is listed individually rather than by practice. There are also other tips to help you find a dentist such as personal recommendations, visiting the practice before making an appointment and talking to the receptionist about emergency cover.

Search the Find-A-Dentist database gives tips for searching the database. You can type in your postcode, county, service required (for example, suitable for children, emergency cover, orthodontics, hypnosis).

Public section leads to dental care tips.

There are some plans for expanding the site's usefulness to the public. It would be a missed opportunity if it didn't as it does not appear to be very extensive.

www.diabetes.org.uk

British Diabetes Organisation

Overall rating: ★★★★

Classification:	Charity	**Readability:**	★★★
Updating:	Regularly	**Reliability:**	★★★★★
Navigation:	★★★	**Speed:**	★★★★

UK

Extensive site from the main UK-based diabetes support charity, the British Diabetic Association (BDA). Here you will find masses of information useful to parents of a newly-diagnosed child or a young adult with diabetes.

SPECIAL FEATURES

Teen zone has lots of good features, such as user-friendly information about hypos (hypoglycaemia), plus details of the BDA's Go For It magazine.

Other features

Access to Diabetic Children in Britain site (currently via Links option: select Parents and children) which is run by the BDA and has a chat room and message board. There are links to other sites via twelve different category headings. One very good link is to the US-based www.childrenwithdiabetes.com.

This is an excellent first port of call for anything on diabetes. There is unlikely to be a more comprehensive site for basic information and contacts.

www.enuresis.org.uk

Enuresis Resource and Information Centre

Overall rating: ★★★★

Classification:	Charity	**Readability:**	★★★★
Updating:	Sometimes	**Reliability:**	★★★★
Navigation:	★★★★★	**Speed:**	★★★★

UK

This is the home site for the UK-based charity ERIC, the Enuresis Resource and Information Centre. The charity provides help, advice and support about bedwetting for parents, health professionals and teenagers.

SPECIAL FEATURES

Facts and figures explains bedwetting and the reasons behind it.

Information for teenagers, of whom 1 in 40 are not yet dry at night.

Other features
Literature and products give details about what is available. There are also contact details about a daily advice line, the ERIC newsletter and other available support.

Links to research sites (Nottingham University) and to practical suppliers such as Huggies, the nappy manufacturers.

Whether you want to check out what is a 'normal' age to be dry at night, or because there is something of a problem and you want to check out what help and support is available, this is the site you need.

www.kidshealth.org

The Nemours Foundation

Overall rating: ★★★★

Classification:	Charity	**Readability:**	★★★★
Updating:	Regularly	**Reliability:**	★★★★
Navigation:	★★★	**Speed:**	★★★★

UK

Produced by the prestigious American healthcare facility, The Nemours Foundation, this is like a huge American reference book with endless articles about different aspects of kid's health. It's for parents, and for kids and teenagers themselves. Choose from a main topic head in each section, which then lists article categories with scroll-down access to article headings for retrieval.

SPECIAL FEATURES

Parents, Kids, and Teens have separate sections, with articles directed at the key reader. For example, under **For Kids** there are 14 articles listed as 'Dealing with Feelings', one of which is A Kid's Guide to Divorce, complete with a helpful booklist.

Cross-referencing There are lots of useful links within articles (in **For Teens**, for example, an article about periods is cross-referenced to one about puberty).

Other features
There is a useful search facility for links to other sites (via the Resources section within each option, and then direct to the website where applicable).

Enormously comprehensive and definitely worth a look.

www.meningitis-trust.org.uk

The National Meningitis Trust

Overall rating: ★★★★

Classification:	Charity	**Readability:**	★★★★
Updating:	Regularly	**Reliability:**	★★★★
Navigation:	★★★★	**Speed:**	★★★★

UK

The National Meningitis Trust's site provides information, complete with a 24-hour helpline number. Concerned parents can check out meningitis symptoms night and day.

SPECIAL FEATURES

Emergency Information provides immediate access to clearly pictured symptoms in adults, children, and babies, with a list of things to do if you suspect meningitis.

What's New section leads to information about the the new meningitis C vaccine.

Youth zone is geared at information for students.

Links to a good range of other sites, including the Department of Health, Dr Mark Porter, Norwich Union (who support the charity), Direct Line (who sponsor the video) and the Meningitis Foundation of America.

This a very good charity website, containing good information about a potentially fatal illness, plus details of research, fundraising and other support activities. There are also case histories.

www.ndcs.org.uk

National Deaf Children's Society

Overall rating: ★★★★

Classification:	Charity	**Readability:**	★★★★
Updating:	Unsure	**Reliability:**	★★★★★
Navigation:	★★★★	**Speed:**	★★★

UK

This is the website for the UK-based National Deaf Children's Society.

SPECIAL FEATURES

Kids' Club comes complete with a virtual art gallery plus requests for contributions which can be emailed direct, a pen-pals scheme, and specific links for kids.

Publications includes NDCS's own magazine, Talk, plus a list of 65 other titles (which range from leaflets on glue ear and sign language to quality standards in paediatric audiology). Facts sheets and leaflets can be ordered or downloaded and read with the benefit of Acrobat Reader.

Regional Network leads to a map of the UK. Highlight any section to receive contact details for NDCS local representatives and groups.

Other features

Try out the message board, **Xpress Yourself.**There is a **How You Can Help** section, with opportunities to take part in NDCS Global Challenges such as cycling in Sri Lanka.

Links to other sites are extensive, covering Education, Deaf Organisations, Government, Further Help and Information.

Excellent! (Though with so many nice graphics and pictures, it is rather slow!)

www.trashed.co.uk

Health Education Authority

Overall rating: ★★★★

Classification:	Government	**Readability:**	★★★★★
Updating:	Regularly	**Reliability:**	★★★★★
Navigation:	★★★★	**Speed:**	★★★★

UK

This is the Health Education Authority's Drugs website. Each drug listed has information about its origins, effects, composition, risks, emergencies, the law (in the UK only) and so on, in an easily accessible form. You need to download RealVideo if you want to view a recording of the website launch in April 1998.

There is also a freephone number for the National Drugs Helpline.

SPECIAL FEATURES

About leads to information on different types of drugs. They can be accessed from a pop-up list, or by typing in the street name and instigating a search ('uppers', for example, will take you to amphetamines). If it can't find your specified request then you can email them for information.

The Law There is up-to-date information regarding the law in this country and this includes categorisation of the different classes of illegal drugs into A, B or C This applies also to the different states of the same drug.

Other features

There is a freephone number for the National Drugs Helpline.

An excellent information site for parents and offspring alike. No doubt it will be popular with teenagers doing Personal and Social Development (PSD) projects at school, too. Unsensational in content and without being judgmental, it just supplies the facts without making it look either 'cool' or censorious.

Also check out www.wrecked.co.uk, a website for teens and young adults on alcohol use and abuse.

www.askyourpharmacist.co.uk

National Pharmaceutical Association

Overall rating: ★★★			
Classification:	Information	**Readability:**	★★★
Updating:	Regularly	**Reliability:**	★★★★★
Navigation:	★★	**Speed:**	★★★★

UK

This is a short, accessible site from the National Pharmaceutical Association. It contains some useful information about taking and storing medicines, plus selected articles on the range of problems with which a pharmacist can help (for example, sun care), with reference to children where applicable.

SPECIAL FEATURES

Directory of pharmacies is a search facility by post code for local pharmacies. This works well – it provided six within a five minutes' walk from a London address.

Kids' page allows pictures to be printed for colouring in – on subjects related to taking medicines.

New this month gives monthly advice on selected topics (for example, stop smoking, constipation and piles, colds and flu, malaria, sport injuries and hay fever).

Links exist to general health information websites and also to specific NHS sites.

www.child.org.uk

The National Infertility Support Network

Overall rating: ★★★			
Classification:	Charity	**Readability:**	★★★★
Updating:	Erratic	**Reliability:**	★★★★★
Navigation:	★★★★	**Speed:**	★★★★

UK

Home site for Child, The National Infertility Support Network, the main UK infertility support group and charity. The site serves mainly as an introduction to the charity's work and as such actively seeks new members.

SPECIAL FEATURES

Membership is encouraged, but not available online. You have to print and send in an order form and cheque. You will then receive details of Child's telephone help line, plus link line to a volunteer when the office is closed. You will also receive Childchat, Child's quarterly magazine.

Fact sheets are listed by title, but have to be ordered direct from the charity.

Links to other infertility websites worldwide, plus academic institutes such as the Royal College of Obstetricians and Gynaecologists, the Department of Health, and so on. Plus the added bonus of websites for two of the charity's patrons, Chris de Burgh and Vivienne Parry!

A good first stop for couples facing infertility and wanting access to good, up-to-date information plus links to other avenues of information. Child are currently advertising for a Webmaster, which would be advantageous to them because there are areas which could be enlarged upon. One small complaint: the music on the site's home page is rather loud!

www.stammering.org

British Stammering Association

Overall rating: ★★★

Classification:	Charity	**Readability:**	★★★
Updating:	Regularly	**Reliability:**	★★★★
Navigation:	★★★	**Speed:**	★★★★

UK

This is the website for the British Stammering Association which looks at what stammering (the UK term – it is known elsewhere as stuttering) is, why it occurs, how speech therapy can help, and how parents can help. There is lots of information on stammering in Pre-school children, School-age children, Teenagers and Young Adults, and Adults. Within the pre-school section there is information for parents of under-fives, in English and Welsh.

SPECIAL FEATURES

Where? What? gives details of the BSA's confidential self-help telephone and counselling groups and their information service.

What's New provides details of courses and conferences this year.

Other features

There are details of books, leaflets and videos for parents, teachers and children which can be obtained direct from the BSA. You can also join the BSA as a member.

Links to a good range of related websites, easily accessed, from around the world.

Very good introductory material for parents who may be wondering if their young child has a problem and what they can do to help. Material is also available in foreign language tapes. Plus good information for school-age and teenage children.

www.hea.org.uk

Health Education Authority

Overall rating: ★★★

Classification:	Government	**Readability:**	★★★
Updating:	Regularly	**Reliability:**	★★★★
Navigation:	★★★	**Speed:**	★★★

UK

A site providing all the information you would expect from the UK's Health Education Authority about what they do, including the research projects which are currently underway.

The site also promotes Healthlines Magazine and gives free sample articles – you can subscribe to it online and it comes through the post.

SPECIAL FEATURES

News and press releases – though not particularly up-to-date. The latest press release was over a month behind.

Health Promotion Information Centre with articles of general interest on public health.

Links to other sites are wide-ranging, from specific websites and across international links to CNN Health, Department of Health press releases, research organisations, and so on, as well as to Dentanet (the online dentist).

This is primarily a site for professionals and there is little of much value to parents, but it provides some good links which may be useful: check out www.lovelife.hea.org.uk, www.thinkfast.co.uk, www.trashed.co.uk, www.wrecked.co.uk, www.immunisation.co.uk.

www.immunisation.org.uk

Health Education Authority

Overall rating: ★★★

Classification:	Government	**Readability:**	★★★
Updating:	Regularly	**Reliability:**	★★★★
Navigation:	★★★	**Speed:**	★★★

UK

This site outlines the childhood immunisation programme in the UK as recommended by the Department of Health. Leaflets and factsheets detailing the full content of HEA information can be downloaded. (The site includes free Acrobat Reader access if needed.) The new meningitis C immunisation is discussed in detail. There is also information on the symptoms of meningitis and septicaemia.

Features include

FAQs for parents keen to know more about immunisations, including DTP (Diptheria, Tetanus, Pertussis/Whooping Cough), Hib (one form of meningitis), Polio, MMR (Measles, Mumps, Rubella), BCG (Tuberculosis) and Hepatitis B.

Links to related charities and information networks such as the British Polio Foundation, to Department of Health press releases and to the World Health Organisation's immunisation pages.

For an opposing view of immunisation, check out the Vaccination Awareness Network's site at www.van.org.uk, but be aware that this is not impartial or medical advice.

Chapter 5

Childcare

For every parent needing some form of baby and childcare, the first hurdle is to discover what options might even be available to you. It is an area of parenting potentially fraught with anxiety, the idea of handing over your precious bundle to another person and, as such, finding the right solution for you and your child demands time and attention. What's more, as your child grows, their needs change: you probably don't need, or want to pay for, a full time nanny if your child or children are at full time school, for example. But finding out what there is in terms of choice can seem an enormous hurdle. No more: it's all on the net, in one form or another. And even those service organisations tend to include broad - based information, while even the DfEE have their stake by including nanny information... Then, when the tables are turned and your almost grown - up child is looking for holiday, gap year, au pair work or a career in childcare, you will still have access to the information you need in order to guide them!

www.dfee.gov.uk/nanny Dept for Education and Employment			
Overall rating: ★★★★			
Classification:	Government	**Readability:**	★★★
Updating:	Regularly	**Reliability:**	★★★★★
Navigation:	★★★★	**Speed:**	★★★
UK			

This is a government site providing advice for parents who are seeking to employ a nanny.

SPECIAL FEATURES

What is a nanny? describes a nanny as someone who is employed to look after your children , in your home usually while you are at work, and they can provide high quality flexible childcare. It categorises different the types of nanny into live-in nannies, daily nannies and nanny-shares.

It also gives details of childminders who usually look after children in their own home and have to be registered to look after children under eight.

Choosing a nanny provides helpful points to consider when drawing up a job description (include duties, hours, driver, non-smoker), when interviewing a nanny and the things to look out for (such as gaps in employment history). Also guidelines on advertising for a nanny and finding the right person, are given. The site reminds prospective employers that because there is no formal nanny register, checking nannies is difficult – there is, for example, no nationally agreed system for the checking of criminal records of people applying for nanny jobs, and warns about looking for gaps in employment history and proof of identity.

Factfile is useful for checking out what childcare qualifications are and what they mean in terms of new national standards. It also provides legal information concerning tax and national insurance considerations, as well as other legalities of employing someone, including household insurance requirements.

Links to other sites are poor as the site only lists contact addresses and telephone numbers for support groups who do have websites, such as the National Childbirth Trust (which isn't entirely appropriate to the subject of nannies),

Although initially this looks very dull and worthy, there is much that is solid, comprehensive and useful for anyone employing a nanny. (There is also information about other sorts of childcare such as au pairs and childminders.) It could certainly do with a more imaginative and accessible lay-out.

www.kidsclubs.com

Kids Club Network

Overall rating: ★★★★

Classification:	Charity	**Readability:**	★★★★
Updating:	Regularly	**Reliability:**	★★★★★
Navigation:	★★★	**Speed:**	★★★

UK

This is the site for Kids' Clubs Network, the UK-based national charity for out-of-school childcare schemes. There are currently 5,500 Kids' Clubs in the UK, registered and inspected by local authorities and aiming to provide after-school and holiday care for four- to twelve-year-olds. Not only does the site provide information for parents, it is a good, carefully selected site for kids.

SPECIAL FEATURES

Find your local club is currently offline, but you can email Kids' Clubs Network to receive a list of clubs closest to you.

Planet Kids is a section specifically for kids, with puzzles, games, educational material, music reviews, and more. It also includes links to TV and film sites (Blue Peter to Warner Bros), to comic sites (such as Spiderman) and to music sites (Spice Girls, Blur, and so on).

Activity ideas section suggests things to do and places to go.

Links Included in the Activity Ideas section is a wide range of approved links to the Star Wars official site, the Science Museum and to the BBC's Newsround site.

www.childcare-info.co.uk

Kids & Co

Overall rating: ★★★

Classification:	Information	**Readability:**	★★★
Updating:	Regularly	**Reliability:**	★★★
Navigation:	★★	**Speed:**	★★★

UK

This website is run by Kids & Co. who aim to provide easily accessible information on childcare related topics and issues.

SPECIAL FEATURES

Choosing the right childcare is a comprehensive section on what to look for when considering a nanny, childminder or nursery. There are also details of how to become a registered childminder, which may be an option for a home-based parent.

Qualifications is a mystifyingly named but informative section on how children learn, the benefits of play, and so on, complete with sections on **Things to Make** and **Things to Cook.**

Childcare agencies provides local authority contacts to approach for information on registered childcare facilities. This is mainly for the London boroughs, but some others are given and there is a commitment to the compilation of a nationwide listing.

Forum includes au pairs looking for work and parents looking for nannies, inbetween requests for information about tax relief on childcare (not available for nannies as they are not registered, which may explain the government's reticence in setting up a formal nanny registration scheme), requests from documentary film makers, and an essay about sleep from a doting dad.

Other features

News and Features section covers items of interest – from the new Childcare Commission to details of the UK's National Bug-Busting day.

Links are extensive and cover a wide variety of areas of interest to parents, including many UK childminders with their own websites!

This is an uncommercial and wide-ranging UK-based site committed to providing information on various aspects of childcare, from finding it to making it interesting for kids.

www.childint.co.uk

Childcare International Ltd

Overall rating: ★★★

Classification:	Agency	**Readability:**	★★★
Updating:	Regularly	**Reliability:**	★★★
Navigation:	★★★	**Speed:**	★★★

UK

Website for the London-based, licensed employment agency Childcare International Ltd, which specialises in international placements for au pairs, mother's helps and nannies and co-operates with agencies worldwide. The site also details what is expected of the different roles, current rates of pay, and so on.

Special Features

Childcare The site provides direct access to finding suitable childcare via the agency. The site is also designed as a source for those trying to find work.

International placements seeks to place au pairs, mother's helps and nannies. The agency offers support for those placed and can provide details of other au pairs living in or near the area of placement.

Links to agencies in mainland Europe, Canada, the US, Australia and South Africa.

A particularly useful site for those wanting nannies for international jobs.

www.daycaretrust.org.uk

Daycare Trust

Overall rating: ★★★

Classification:	Charity	**Readability:**	★★★
Updating:	Regularly	**Reliability:**	★★★★★
Navigation:	★★★	**Speed:**	★★★

UK

The Daycare Trust is the UK-based national childcare campaign, working towards high-quality childcare for all. It is also a membership organisation. As a charity, its remit includes information dissemination and this is where it excels. Not only can the Daycare Trust be contacted via its childcare hotline, there is also an email address.

SPECIAL FEATURES

Choosing childcare Comprehensive and up-to-date information about all the childcare options available in the UK, from nannies and playgroups to early education and after-school clubs. There are good ideas for how to find childcare and details of what resources are available to parents, particularly via local authorities. There are also good suggestions about what parents need to consider and check out when selecting childcare.

Becoming a working parent (under the **Choosing Childcare** option) is a useful guide which covers both the practical and emotional details, including maternity rights legislation.

Paying for childcare is an extremely valuable section which will help to guide parents through some of the recent legislation (such as the Childcare Tax Credit).

Childcare help for students offers unique information about the facilities that may be available to students who need to organise childcare.

Other features

Details of a childcare hotline available (10 am to 5 pm Monday to Friday).

Links to other sites are provided within the body of the copy, not as a separate section. Covers a selected number only (the National Childminding Association, Kids' Clubs Network, appropriate Government departments and the Inland Revenue).

www.family-match.com

Family Match

Overall rating: ★★★

Classification:	Agency	**Readability:**	★★★
Updating:	Weekly	**Reliability:**	★★★
Navigation:	★★★	**Speed:**	★★★

UK

Family Match is one of the UK's leading nanny agencies.

SPECIAL FEATURES

Information for clients provides details such as current rates of pay, interview questions, 20 helpful tips for employers of nannies, a sample contract, and so on.

Information for nannies provides details of what the agency expects – a useful way for parents to see the selection process. There is also information for English-speakers from abroad.

Situations vacant gives a useful idea of how your vacancy might be advertised through the agency.

Ski, sun and cruise page provides cost and advice on hiring a holiday nanny for a private family and also for nannies looking for jobs with travel companies (ski or sun).

Other features

Application form to print out and fax as well as a very useful tax calculator form. Most nannies are paid net, so you can look up the total cost to the employer.

Links to a range of sites, including the UK Government's guide for parents, Upmystreet, Kids and Co and nanny colleges.

Although limited geographically (serving mainly South-East England), this is a good site for parents who are just starting the childcare trawl because it gives such good advice for those inexperienced at selecting childcare.

www.iapa.org

Internation Au Pair Association

Overall rating: ★★★			
Classification:	Agency	**Readability:**	★★★
Updating:	Occasionally	**Reliability:**	★★★
Navigation:	★★	**Speed:**	★★★

UK

The 'official' website for the International Au Pair Association based in Denmark. Designed primarily as an umbrella organisation for the industry, it gives a full list of the international agencies and organisations who are affiliated members. It doesn't arrange placements, but provides details of registered members who can.

SPECIAL FEATURES

Membership agencies The site provides a good list of international members (84 in 29 countries) complete with contact details.

Other features

There are useful details of what can be expected of an au pair, and what an au pair can expect of their host family and how to avoid conflict.

Good introductory information about how to find and employ an au pair.

www.nanniesinc.com

Nannies Incorporated

Overall rating: ★★★			
Classification:	Agency	**Readability:**	★★★
Updating:	Occasionally	**Reliability:**	★★★
Navigation:	★★★	**Speed:**	★★★

UK

An easy and straightforward website for Nannies Incorporated, an international nanny agency, established for over ten years and with offices in London and Paris. It provides information on how nannies and maternity nurses are recruited and placed, gives details of fees, and so on. Email contact is possible but personal phone contact is needed for registration and to discuss needs.

SPECIAL FEATURES

Our nannies explains the agency's approach and provides representative samples of some of their nanny's CVs.

Our maternity nurses does the same for maternity nurses for newborn babies.

Information and access to a leading nanny and maternity nurse agency, skilled at providing placements worldwide.

www.nannyjob.co.uk

Nanny Job

Overall rating: ★★★

Classification:	Information	**Readability:**	★★★
Updating:	Daily	**Reliability:**	★★★★
Navigation:	★★	**Speed:**	★★★

UK

A free internet service for the childcare sector, this site gives extensive access to directories and information – from publications on childcare to addresses and nanny job news.

SPECIAL FEATURES

Seeking work? There is an option to submit a vacancy (by filling in a form online and posting direct to their database), search for jobs, submit to and search for a CV database. There are also helpful tips and fact sheets (such as Au Pair Explained). The search for jobs is extensive – for example 'nanny, London' threw up 181 vacancies but only two-line descriptions of each. Response is by direct email to the advertiser. However, over 500 vacancies are advertised but there are currently only 100 CVs posted by nannies.

Directories Search the agency's database for a childcare agency or nursery in every region of the UK.

Links to an extensive variety of childcare and recruitment sites, plus advertisers such as amazon.co.uk.

Good site both for parents considering all aspects of childcare and also for those wishing to find work looking after children.

www.nannytax.co.uk

Nannytax

Overall rating: ★★★

Classification:	Information	**Readability:**	★★★★
Updating:	Regularly	**Reliability:**	★★★★
Navigation:	★★★★	**Speed:**	★★★★

UK

Nannytax is primarily a payroll service for anyone who employs a nanny and who is required by law to fulfill certain obligations as an employer.

SPECIAL FEATURES

Employer information details everything a parent employing a nanny needs to know about their legal obligations.

Nanny information provides tax and national insurance information for nannies.

Other features

Direct contact can be made for a fuller information pack. There is a link to the Tinies Nanny Agency.

A straightforward, no-nonsense site providing information with no frills.

www.ncma.org.uk
The National Childminding Association

Overall rating: ★★★

Classification:	Agency	**Readability:**	★★★
Updating:	Regularly	**Reliability:**	★★★★
Navigation:	★★★	**Speed:**	★★★

UK

This is the website for the National Childminding Association, the UK-based support organisation for registered childminders, of whom there are 100,000 in this country. Although the site is designed primarily for childminders, it is a good source of information for parents who want to know what this excellent form of childcare can provide.

SPECIAL FEATURES

Childminders The site details information about childminders, how they work and how to find a registered childminder. It also outlines the Quality Standards integral to childminding practice.

Publications The NCMA produces numerous publications and audio tapes (Playsongs, for example), many of which are primarily for childminders. But there is also a good booklet for parents entitled Choosing a Childminder which is available direct.

Training Look here for details of the NCMA's training course, Developing Childminding Practice, which links to an NVQ level 3 in Early Years Education.

The site is still in development, but it already meets a need for information on childminding and can only go from strength to strength.

www.norland.co.uk
The Norland Nanny College

Overall rating: ★★

Classification:	Agency	**Readability:**	★★★
Updating:	Sometimes	**Reliability:**	★★★★
Navigation:	★★★★	**Speed:**	★★★★

UK R

Primarily a website for the Norland Nanny training college, this provides prospective employers details of what the training involves and how to go about employing a Norland nanny.

SPECIAL FEATURES

Employment provides information about the Norland registry, Norland's own international employment agency. The registry holds a list of potential employers.

Training Find details of childcare and education (three months to eleven years) facilities provided on-site at the Norland training college, situated between Hungerford and Newbury in Berkshire, England.

Limited in scope as it is purely a brochure for the college.

www.nursery-world.com

Nursery World

Overall rating: ★★

Classification:	Magazine	**Readability:**	★★★
Updating:	Regularly	**Reliability:**	★★★
Navigation:	★★★	**Speed:**	★★★

UK

Primarily for professional childcare workers, this is the site for the weekly magazine Nursery World, published by News International.

SPECIAL FEATURES

Editorial provides selected summarised features from almost a year's worth of Nursery World back issues.

So You Want to Employ a Nanny? is a good, comprehensive article about how to start.

Jobs provides opportunities for advertisers including parents looking for childcare.

Other features

Direct contact is available to Nursery World's help desk. The site also offers a small selection of books, primarily for professional childcare workers. These are available for direct sale via the Times Educational Supplement book-buying service.

Links to site advertisers such as www.learnfree.co.uk and www.webnannies.com, for example.

Limited interest to parents, but useful for an overview of childcare issues provided by its selected editorial culled from the magazine.

www.webnannies.com

Childcare Services Ltd

Overall rating: ★★

Classification:	Agency	**Readability:**	★★
Updating:	Monthly	**Reliability:**	★★★
Navigation:	★	**Speed:**	★★★

UK

This is the site for Childcare Services Ltd, primarily an au pair/nanny agency. It is divided into two sections, Families and Home Help (although this takes you to identical material) and is designed to be informative for both nannies and prospective employers.

SPECIAL FEATURES

Information for nannies is a comprehensive guide on all aspects of nanny care.

Information for families provides an introduction to nannies, home helps and au pairs.

Chat rooms are promised shortly for nannies and families, in addition to a Nanny Share register.

Latest news section has some interesting articles, for nannies and parents alike, on parental leave, family health, summer au pairs, national minimum wage, and so on.

Police checks There are details of how a prospective nanny can have a police check done on herself at a cost of £10.00. The check takes 40 days to complete.

Other features

A monthly book review (which would be better served by including a feature on reading to children and linking to a book service such as amazon.co.uk).

Links to sites such as the St John's Ambulance, who can provide First Aid training, as recommended to all prospective nannies.

Although it does have some useful features, and is useful as an agency, as a site this could benefit from development. It is very tricky to move around.

Chapter 6

Education

In many ways, the abiding preoccupation of parents (after health) is the education of their children. This section encompasses education in its broadest sense: from finding a school to helping with homework. Thankfully, this is one area of the net where there is a wealth of assistance. It is now possible to get information about every school in the UK, plus their Ofsted report, and how they performed in the league tables. All this information and choice, however, doesn't guarantee getting a particular school place for your child, which is why charities like the Advisory Centre for Education are also included.

Choosing Schools and Universities

When it comes to choosing a school, or selecting a college or university course, information is key. While this has always been available if you knew where to look, it wasn't always easily accessible, and this where the internet provides a fantastic resource. Instead of trawling through endless bits and pieces of diverse information, once you have accessed a site, search facilities make it simple.

www.goodschoolsguide.co.uk

The Good Schools Guide

Overall rating: ★★★★★

Classification:	Information	**Readability:**	★★★★
Updating:	Frequently	**Reliability:**	★★★★
Navigation:	★★★★	**Speed:**	★★★★

UK £ R

This is the very informative website from The Good Schools Guide team (headed by the Editor, Amanda Atha) which gives personal and unbiased reviews and information about the top schools in the UK.

You can view examples of the schools' reviews for free, currently Eton and Hill House International Junior School, which make entertaining, as well as informative, reading! However, you have to subscribe to have access to the full content of the Good Schools Guide, available for an annual fee of £17.99 and for this you can request a free copy of their book. The independent and impartial guide gives vivid descriptions, plus lots of advice about each school which makes the Guide's review of a school invaluable. The online reviews are regularly updated.

SPECIAL FEATURES

The Subscribers Area is available only for those who have subscribed (which you can do instantly, online). It divides into sections:

Introductory Chapters includes advice on **How to Read this Book** (advising you to read between the lines of the reviews), **Entry procedures** (visiting, registering, entry exams), **What the League Tables Don't Tell You** (such as about the pupil's backgrounds, the school's background – is it Selective or Mixed Ability – their policy on 6th forms and other important issues), **Sussing Out a School** gives advice on what to look out for and a list of over 50 questions to ask. There are also important chapters on **Money Matters** (advice on scholarships, bursaries, assisted places and other matters connected to paying the fees for private schools) they do suggest asking for a discount if you have more than two children at a school.

The Good Schools Guide Advisory Service is a consultancy, run by the Good Schools Guide, which can help parents find the right school to match their child's needs, for a standard fee of £150. For this they specialise in matching the child with a school, giving inside information on what a school is really like, suggesting good schools that you may not know about, checking out specific schools for you and information on strong specialist departments and unusual features. If you really do not know much about the UK independent school system or if your child does not fit into the mainstream for some reason then this might be useful.

There are also informative, short book reviews dotted around the site, linked to Amazon.co.uk and other excellent links divided into sub-sections: Advice, Exam Boards, Further Education, The Gap Year, Government, Moving Home, News, Resources, Schools Lists and Guides, Summer Schools, and Universities.

The Good Schools Guide site provides a personal and independent review of the 'top' UK schools, and covers mainly fee-paying schools, with the occasional foray into the state system. That said, it also provides pointers to how to work the fee-paying system to your best advantage, including considerations of scholarships, bursaries, and how to decipher schools' own (often biased) information. This is an essential stop if you are considering sending your child to a private school or are concerned about getting your child into a top state school.

www.dfee.gov.uk

The Department for Education and Employment

Overall rating: ★★★★

Classification:	Government	**Readability:**	★★★★
Updating:	Regularly	**Reliability:**	★★★★★
Navigation:	★★★★	**Speed:**	★★★★

UK

The Department for Education and Employment's site provides access to performance tables for all UK schools. You can go to the very straightforward site index and click on the alphabetical index to get easy access to information.

SPECIAL FEATURES

Site index leads to an alphabetical list of all DfEE documents held at the site. For example, under 'I' find 'It's Your Choice' with education and training choices at 16, plus information about exam technique, tips and golden rules for revision.

News provides access to all press releases and publications put out by the DfEE, primarily for teachers and educationalists. There is also a news search facility. Where documents can be downloaded, the site provides appropriate software.

Links to 18 related sites outside the DfEE, including the Advisory Centre for Education, Ofsted, New Deal and Careers Research. Plus Connexions, a links website divided into Young People, Parents/Guardians, Employers and Professional Practitioners. This provides excellent links to related, though not necessarily educational, websites.

Although a UK Government site, providing lots of details about education in the UK, there is much more on this site of value. Useful to parents of school-age children from 5 to 18, and beyond.

www.hobsons.co.uk Hobsons			
Overall rating: ★★★★			
Classification:	Information	**Readability:**	★★★
Updating:	Regularly	**Reliability:**	★★★
Navigation:	★★★★	**Speed:**	★★★
UK			

A global career and education service, this British and US-based company has over 25 years' experience in publishing educational and recruitment guides for students making career and course decisions. The content is diverse, from upbeat student information to the hard graft of making decisions about further education or work.

SPECIAL FEATURES

Home page is split into Education or Careers. Take it from there for introductory information and how to find out more.

Springboard student services provides careers, education and lifestyle information for 16-18 year olds and benefits from an Advertisers section where organisations ranging from Orange, Budgens, Volkswagen, the RAF, Mencap, IBM, the Careers and Occupation Information Centre, and more, advertise and outline their career opportunities.

Links to the five main aspects of this site: Whichuni (find a university), Coursenet (locate a course), StudyUK, Boarding (guide to UK boarding schools) and Ecctis (UK course information service). Links to other sites also exist within the body of the text. For example, find Kate Moss within Lifestyle and there are links to her site. Similarly for the Storm model agency, JFK airport, Calvin Klein, Johnny Depp, Vogue and others.

One benefit of the site is that it manages to combine facts with upbeat background information. For example, information about careers in media includes a detailed day-in-the-life of film director Jim Gillespie, a feature which gives good insight into what glamorous-sounding jobs actually consist of and how to go about getting there! However, there's still room for a more comprehensive overview of career choices, and this is an area the site could do well to develop. Also note that it does take a bit of time to connect to specific sites within the main site.

www.schoolsnet.com

Schools Net

Overall rating: ★★★★

Classification:	Information	**Readability:**	★★★★
Updating:	Regularly	**Reliability:**	★★★★
Navigation:	★★★★	**Speed:**	★★★

UK

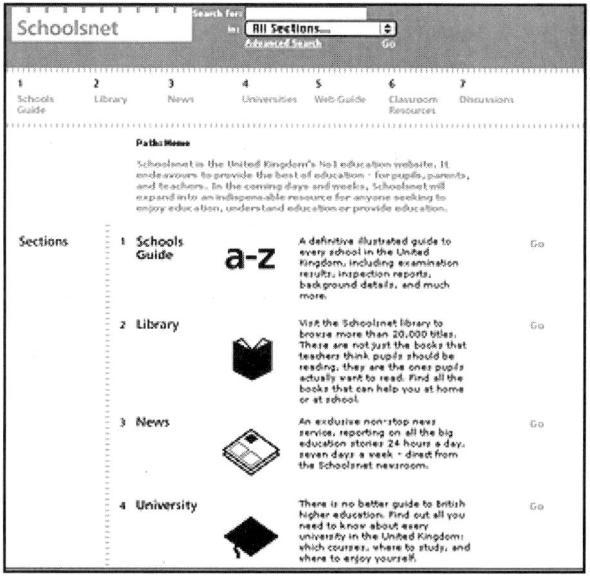

This is an excellent, UK-based website aiming to meet very clear needs by supplying extensive information on schools and universities, plus a library, news service, and more.

SPECIAL FEATURES

Schools Guide is described as a definitive, illustrated guide to every school and university in the UK (including examination results, inspection reports and background details). Although this coverage isn't yet complete the basic information is there.

Library Visit an illustrated library of more than 20,000 titles.

News concentrates on educational stories compiled by Schoolsnet in-house journalists.

Classroom resources for pupils and teachers, including interactive lessons, essay plans and exam questions.

Links to a well organised Web Guide, by 18 subject categorisations (for example, art, modern languages, science, and so on).

The site was only launched in November 1999, and although the basics are there it will undoubtedly improve with time as more information (for example, in the classroom resources section) is added.

www.ucas.co.uk

Universities and Colleges Admissions Service

Overall rating: ★★★★

Classification:	Information	**Readability:**	★★★★
Updating:	Regularly	**Reliability:**	★★★★
Navigation:	★★★★★	**Speed:**	★★★★

UK £ R

This is the website for the Universities and Colleges Admissions Service. It provides comprehensive and up-to-date information about all university and college courses throughout the UK and is designed for use by students and schools or colleges, with a direct line to each one's website.

SPECIAL FEATURES

Universities, colleges, courses contains a well-organised and easy-to-use **Course Search** option that finds which courses are available.

Advice centre for prospective students and parents as well as schools and colleges, answers questions about seeking a course, it also provides financial advice.

Links includes for applicants and students, for teachers and support staff, and for higher education staff. Students links include the National Union of Students, Student Loans Company, and the British Library. There is a direct link to studentuk.com with a good news and advice section. plus **You Can** an interesting section produced by UCAS and The Independent newspaper

In addition, this site also takes advantage of the fact that students and prospective students will be logging on and provides a lot of student-friendly advice and information which is well worth a browse.

www.ofsted.gov.uk

Office For Standard in Education

Overall rating: ★★★

Classification:	Government	**Readability:**	★★★★
Updating:	Monthly	**Reliability:**	★★★★
Navigation:	★★★★	**Speed:**	★★★★

UK £ R

UK-based site providing access to Ofsted (Office for Standards in Education) reports. Ofsted is a non-ministerial government department, independent from the Department for Education and Employment (DfEE), and is the official office of Her Majesty's Chief Inspector for Schools in England, set up in September 1992 more information is given in **About Ofsted** .There is also a section of **publications** and **press releases** with relevant news items.

SPECIAL FEATURES

Nursery Reports gives details of every Local Education Authority's Early Years Development Plan for four year olds in order to provide a free place for those whose parents want one. There is also detailed reports about the inspections of private, voluntary, and independent nursery education settings as well as inspection reports from the state sector nursery schools.

School reports lead to access to the Ofsted reports of every school in the country.

Teacher-training courses which have to undergo Ofsted, are also listed at this site.

A very good site with clear information for those wanting to look up a specific report.

Year By Year Guide To Schooling

AGE OF CHILD	UK TYPE OF SCHOOL	UK EDUCATIONAL CLASS	NATIONAL CURRICULUM STAGE	USA GRADE	US TYPE OF SCHOOL
3 - 4 years	Nursery				
4 - 5 years	Infants	Reception	Key Stage 1		Kindergarten
5 - 6 years		Year 1			
6 - 7 years		Year 2		Grade 1	Elementary
7 - 8 years	Junior	Year 3	Key Stage 2	Grade 2	
8 - 9 years		Year 4		Grade 3	
9 - 10 years		Year 5		Grade 4	
10 - 11 years		Year 6		Grade 5	
11 - 12 years	Senior	Year 7	Key Stage 3	Grade 6	Junior High - Middle School
12 - 13 years		Year 8		Grade 7	
13 - 14 years		Year 9		Grade 8	
14 - 15 years		Year 10	GCSE	Grade 9	High School - Freshman
15 - 16 years	GCSE year	Year 11		Grade 10	High School - Sophmore
16 - 17 years	6th Form	Year 12	A Levels	Grade 11	High School - Juniors
17 - 18 years	A Level year	Year 13		Grade 12	High School - Seniors

Educational Issues

Finding an appropriate school, college or university for your child may be simple, but sometimes issues arise concerning your choice. What if you have appeal for a school place, how do you go about it? Or, if there are issues about the home-school contract, or how to become a school governor, how can you find out more? Numerous sites, like that for the Times Educational Supplement, cover issues to do with education, while the Advisory Centre for Education is exactly that, an advice centre for parents.

www.educationunlimited.co.uk

The Guardian Newspaper

Overall rating: ★★★★★

Classification:	Newspaper	**Readability:**	★★★★★
Updating:	Daily	**Reliability:**	★★★★★
Navigation:	★★★★	**Speed:**	★★★★

UK

This is the education site for the Guardian and Observer newspapers. It has good sectionds for Parents, schools, Colleges, and so on, plus online news from the papers themselves.

SPECIAL FEATURES

Parents section leads to, for example, Choosing a school, Homework help, and Net nannies (the latter providing links to sites designed to inform you about, and protect your child from some of the worst aspects of the net).

Books section provides recommendations by age, plus online ordering with bol.com.

News provides access to education news stories, as they have appeared in these papers, and has a search facility.

Links to other sites only through the different sections.

www.parents.dfee.gov.uk

The Department for Education and Employment

Overall rating: ★★★★★

Classification:	Government	**Readability:**	★★★★
Updating:	Regularly	**Reliability:**	★★★★★
Navigation:	★★★★	**Speed:**	★★★★

UK R

A site directed at helping parents with their child's education. It opens with a Welcome to the Parents' Centre page. There are click through buttons, In School, Out of School and one to Personalise (register) in order to highlight information relevant to you. If you are a first-time user you need to click on this button which takes you through very basic instructions on using the internet and on using this site, and then to a registration page for details of yourself and your children.

SPECIAL FEATURES

In School tells you what your child is learning, information about the National Curriculum, about Home/School Agreements, that chance to see what Key Stage assessments involve, and so on.

Out of School gives advice on choosing a school, plus information about home learning, gifted children's needs, parents' organisations and support groups, what to do if you aren't offered a place at the school of your choice... it's all here.

School Seach leads to a searchable database of DfEE Performance Tables, School Website Database and the Ofsted School Reports all rolled into one. If you enter your postcode, and whether you're interested in primary or secondary level, it gives you a list of schools in your area. For each school you can see background information (number of pupils and number of SEN pupils), Key Stage 2 test results for the previous year (with and without SEN) broken into English, Maths and Science and a Measure of Improvement table so you can see how the school has improved against itself, against its Local Education Authority and Nationally.

Places to Go gives great, nationwide information about activities, functions, sites and places of interest throughout the UK. For example, key in 'Colchester' and 59 results are returned, including a clock museum, Colchester castle, a three-storey adventure playground, nature reserve and a railway museum.

Other features

News option links you not only to DfEE press releases, but also to the BBC, ITN, Sky, The Guardian, Guardian Education, Times, Telegraph, Independent, Daily Mail, Mirror, Star, Express and the Times Educational Supplement.

A search facility, enables you to find out something when you're not sure where to look, for example, type in 'I'd like to know more about English and drama subjects' and it will take you to the appropriate area of the Parents' Centre.

There are links to other sites divided into five key groups: Choices post-16, Curriculum Support, Health and Welfare, Government and Agencies, and Support Groups.

This is an unexpectedly useful site, especially if you are looking at various local schools and how they are doing. It is also useful for all aspects of parenting that concern education in its widest sense, both in and out of school.

www.tes.co.uk

Times Educational Supplement online

Overall rating: ★★★★

Classification:	Newspaper	**Readability:**	★★★★
Updating:	Weekly	**Reliability:**	★★★★
Navigation:	★★★★	**Speed:**	★★★★

UK

This is the online version of The Times Educational Supplement, (part of News International newspaper group and also accessible via www.thetimes.co.uk) with its free access (no registration or subscription required), which also benefits from other online features of interest to teachers, and parents of children currently in fulltime education up to school leaving age.

SPECIAL FEATURES

Current Edition is free access to articles and features available online as well as those only available in this weeks printed edition of the TES.

TES online option takes you to information about computers in education, complete with features and reviews, plus information about free educational downloads and a weekly comment by the Online editor.

Theatre For Schools provides a guide to theatre for young people, a drama and information service for schools to help you make choices about which theatre companies to book and what plays to see, whether you are a student or a teacher. This is divided up into sections as follows: **Theatre in Education** is a listing of participatory theatre groups who tour to schools and colleges; **Theatre for Young People** is a listing of touring companies involved in young children's plays; **Youth Theatre Companies** is a directory; **Workshops for Teachers** gives a list of drama workshops, **Mainhouse Productions** is where you click here for theatre previews, a guide to repertory and touring productions. There is also a **Theatre Reviews** archive from the previous year.

Primary magazine is a monthly magazine with features and articles on various issues such as a teacher's guide to special needs children, which is long article (lots of scrolling down) about dealing with children suffering from a number of difficulties such as autism, emotional and behavioural difficulties, dyslexia, dyspraxia, hearing and vision impairment, plus subscription details.

Governors pages provides support for school governors, whether parent governors or otherwise, with a selection of archive articles such as school inspections and frequent questions and answers. There is also advice on how to become a Governor, on the National Curriculum, on the National Association of Governors and Managers and the National Governors Council plus a briefing forum and links to useful websites (ie. the DfEE site, Becoming a Governor).

Other features

These include The TES bookshop which contains a small selection of books covering education, available to purchase direct from the TES online, with a secure ordering facility, a TES archive, with search facility, for articles going back to 1994. There are also links to specialist education websites divided into sections including curriculum, schools, research, local authorities, special needs, etc.

Primarily a site of interest to teachers, it also provides a good resource for parents interested in education, especially if they want information about being a parent governor. As part of the News International group, it is possible to access individual sites, via www.thetimes.co.uk, for The Times, The Sunday Times, The Sun, News of the World, The Times Higher Educational Supplement, The Times Literary Supplement as well as the TES. While the designated educational sites provide much of value and interest, it's also worth trawling through the features departments of the main newspapers for new items and features relevant to parenting and education.

ACE
ADVISORY CENTRE FOR EDUCATION

Home About ACE Questions & Answers Discussion Governors & Community Publications Other Sites

Welcome to the ACE Web Site.

On this site, you will find news and information specifically for parents, school governors and teachers.
ACE produce many useful leaflets and publications which are available to buy through the Publications Page.
You can also support ACE by subscribing to the Stop Press or ACE Bulletin or by becoming a Member. Follow the link below for more information.

Please sign our Guest Book

View the News and Information Page

Become a Member of ACE

How To Reach Us

Advisory Centre For Education (ACE) LTD
Department A
Unit 1C Aberdeen Studios
22 Highbury Grove
London
N5 2DQ

www.ace-ed.org.uk

The Advisory Centre for Education

Overall rating: ★★★

Classification:	Charity	**Readability:**	★★★★
Updating:	Monthly	**Reliability:**	★★★★★
Navigation:	★★★★	**Speed:**	★★★★

UK

This is the UK-based site for The Advisory Centre for Education (ACE), an independent national advice centre for parents, school governors and teachers, and a registered charity. It's aim is to help parents help their children at school by providing advice on education law and also a sympathetic ear, enabling parents to deal with issues, usually when things go wrong.

SPECIAL FEATURES

Publications leads to a good range of books and information sheets for parents, school governors and schools. All can be ordered direct.

Discussion forum Questions and Answers are dealt with by ACE's expert staff. They suggest you look at the FAQs first and email them if you don't find what you need. They aim to provide answers to specific questions in 48 hours.

FAQs for example, about where schools should stand legally on dyslexia or, autism, christianity and church schools, and bullying. Updated regularly.

Links to a selected few including DfEE, Ofsted, Mentors in School Networks, and the ADD/ADHD Family Support Group.

A good site,which is easy to navigate as the site index remains on each page.

Learning Resources

Education at school is only half of it: there are a multiplicity of sites designed to assist your child with all sorts of aspects of their school work, plus access to sites like Discovery, BBC Education, and the National Gallery to broaden their horizon. In addition, not only can you find details of university courses throughout the UK, but also throughout the world's universities.

www.bbc.co.uk/education

BBC Online

Overall rating: ★★★★★

Classification:	Information	**Readability:**	★★★★
Updating:	Regularly	**Reliability:**	★★★★★
Navigation:	★★★★	**Speed:**	★★★★

UK

Here you'll find sites for BBC programmes in transmission. Look, for example, for Teletubbies for 0-3 year olds or Tweenies for 3-5 year olds. Both have educational factors, games to play, tips about reading, and so on. If you jump to Kids, you get Blue Peter and Newsround, which provide added value and back-up to the programmes.

SPECIAL FEATURES

Schools section contains resources for primary- and secondary-school children and for home learning. Information on literacy, numeracy, the national curriculum key stages, figure prominently.

Science section is linked to BBC programmes such as Tomorrow's World and Horizon, but also has sections on the basics, such as the Human Body.

Other features

Other sections worth checking out include Languages, the Learning Zone, Health and History. Also take time to visit the Web Guide section, a directory to over 3,000 of the best websites for learning, complete with category sections and a search option. Within each section there are useful links.

Navigation and speed around the site are pretty good considering how vast it is. This site is almost worth the television licence fee alone! I can't rate it highly enough, just go see it!

www.booktrust.org.uk The Book Trust			
Overall rating: ★★★★★			
Classification:	Charity	**Readability:**	★★★★
Updating:	Regularly	**Reliability:**	★★★★★
Navigation:	★★★★	**Speed:**	★★★
UK			

This is a truly wonderful site from the UK-based charity, the Book Trust, an organisation designed to promote books and reading and encourage readers of all ages. The Book Trust aims to help readers, parents, teachers, librarians, reading groups, media, writers and the book industry.

SPECIAL FEATURES

Young Book Trust gives good advice for parents here about introducing books to young children and encouraging reading, plus details of how to order the age-specific parents' pack from the Book Trust, complete with a free copy of 100 Best Books.

Bookstart is a project in development over two years which aims to introduce babies to books by giving a free pack at a baby's 9 month health check. It is sponsored by Sainsburys (hence a link to their site) and the pack will include two specially selected board books. There will also be advice on further titles for babies and toddlers, an action rhyming placement and lots of useful information on how to enjoy books with children.

Book lists of recommended books by age group, from first books for babies, to newly fluent readers, to reluctant readers, to teenage fiction.

Other features

The site provides details of author appearances, literary festivals, and forthcoming book awards, plus contact details for children's book publishers. There is a FAQ section which is essentially a database of information about how to find books, publishers and other subjects.

Links to a range of book-related organisations such as the Library Association, the British Library, Publishing News, and The Bookseller. The obvious link, which it doesn't have, would be to an online bookseller!

This is a clear and very readable site, as you might expect from the Book Trust. One for book-lovers everywhere.

www.discovery.com

The Discovery Channel

Overall rating: ★★★★★

Classification:	TV channel	**Readability:**	★★★★
Updating:	Regularly	**Reliability:**	★★★★★
Navigation:	★★★★	**Speed:**	★★★★

US

This is the television channel's website, with extensive information about the natural world, the environment, and more. It is divided into seven main sections: Discoveries, Health, Pets, Travel, Lifestyles, School and Kids. If you download RealPlayer for free you can watch some features (for which all times are given as ET, or east coast of America).

SPECIAL FEATURES

Channels Visit enables you to visit Discovery's different television channels. For example, if you go to the Science channel where you'll find an extensive range of good science-based features, from prehistoric sharks to modern health.

Kids section leads to on-screen games with interactive features, including building a roller coaster, saving a sea turtle and spotting a UFO. You are sent to a huge list of adventure pages such as growing a salad from seeds and eating them. It encourages you to do some research beforehand and gives guidelines on useful websites. You can make your own personal list of favourites.

discoveryschool.com gives channels for teachers,students and parents. **Teachers** gives lesson plans, videos links and other useful resources. **Students** aims to help with homework by providing their selection of the best links, for example there is a searchable database of information on regions, countries and cities around the world. **Parents** gives advice on educational videos and software as well as explanations of the homework help resources.

Search facility provides wide-ranging access to site topics, plus others.

Discovery Store is the site's online shopping facility, available to international customers with an appropriate credit card. A secure server is used for this. Additional costs for transportation are incurred and some restrictions on products do apply. It sells a wide range of videos and science related objects ranging from astronomy tools (including telescopes), jewellery (including gemstones), and scale models (World War I and II aircraft, and classic cars from the 1950's). You can register for a passport card to collect loyalty points.

Links occur only to associated sites. For example, there is a direct link to www.school.discovery.com where you'll find three sections: for Teachers, Students and Parents. It provides good school and homework back-up.

Much more than merely an information site to provide added value to the satellite television channel, as could be expected from an outfit with Discovery's expertise. This is a great site.

www.gcse.com GCSE Answers Ltd			
Overall rating: ★★★★★			
Classification:	Information	**Readability:**	★★★
Updating:	Daily	**Reliability:**	★★★★★
Navigation:	★★★★	**Speed:**	★★★★
UK £ R			

The primary aim of GCSE Answers Ltd, the owners of this UK-based site, lies in their focus on answering problems students may be having with GCSE Maths and English, but the site is much more than just this. It is a well thought out support system for students, parents and teachers alike, providing comprehensive description and support for the GCSE courses and exams.

It is an award-winning site and an approved content provider for the DfE's National Grid for Learning. However, lots of multi-coloured text (used to break up the page) makes it slightly wearing. Also note that, although no special software is required for this site, the home page suggests that there are many advanced features so you should ensure you have updated versions of browsers.

SPECIAL FEATURES

Your Questions, Our Answers provides a good introduction for students and parents who are not sure how to use this site.

Tutorials Basic tutorials lead to more advanced work. All of these are devised to provide added support to school teaching.

Easy start provides a good basic guide to maths from the beginning.

Email link to the site through which you can raise specific questions.

Links to other sites, include GCSE Examining Boards, Support for students (which ranges from Britannia History and Henry Cordy's Biology Pages to Jane Austen's Corner and Mr Maths – and more), Support for parents (including Education Otherwise, the British Dyslexia Association, and Cambridge Learning), Educational resources and support for teachers, Teachers trade unions, and Government authorities.

The site is organised by teachers and academics – and they appear to know their stuff, making it an invaluable stop for parents trying to work out how best to help their offspring.

www.learnfree.co.uk

Learnfree

Overall rating: ★★★★★

Classification:	Information	**Readability:**	★★★
Updating:	Regularly	**Reliability:**	★★★★
Navigation:	★★★	**Speed:**	★★★★

UK

Supported by the Times Educational Supplement, this UK-based site is designed to provide help for learners of all ages, opportunities for parents to be more fully involved with their child's education, and practical help for teachers.

SPECIAL FEATURES

Learners, parents and teachers are all provided with separate, easily accessible sections.

Learning and teaching material The site provides a wealth of specially-commissioned ideas for approaches to all subjects.

Curriculum guide (in the parents section) leads parents through what is expected for all the National Curriculum key stages, including pre-school plus GCSEs and A levels.

University Guide complete with ratings from the Times Higher Educational Supplement, plus a really good introduction which covers things to consider when making a choice. Good information about finance, too.

Other features

There are useful book reviews. It is also possible to email the editor if you cannot find what you're looking for. And take a look at Best of the Web, a section which is full of good links for a wide range of subjects, including performance tables, schools throughout the UK with websites, texts of educational documents, international media, information about school governors, international educational organisations, learning games and revision.

One very good link for university information is push online at www.push.co.uk. There are also links to amazon.co.uk, bol.com and Waterstones Online – all of which are useful for ordering recommended books, and those from the Try It/Buy It section direct – plus links to advertisers such as lastminute.com.

This site is a minefield of information and provides the most comprehensive links any parent could wish for! There is a good site map. However, the site is slow, mainly because the Try it/Buy it section requires Acrobat Reader (which can be downloaded free) to read the book extracts.

www.louvre.fr

The Louvre

Overall rating: ★★★★★			
Classification:	Gallery	**Readability:**	★★★★
Updating:	Regularly	**Reliability:**	★★★★★
Navigation:	★★★★	**Speed:**	★★★

FR

This excellent site from the famous Louvre museum in Paris provides a fantastic array of items from the museum's collections for you to view online, from paintings to sculpture. The homepage opens in French but you can switch to English, Spanish or Japanese. The site is divided up into:

Palace Museum, with the history of the museum and the collections.

Activities, gives details of forthcoming exhibitions and guided tours.

SPECIAL FEATURES

Discover our virtual tour around nine different galleries within the Louvre (this requires the software programme Quick-Time4 which can be downloaded from the Apple website, a facility included on the page). This gives you a fantastic overview of the major works of art and where in the gallery they are located. We would certainly recommend a look before a visit.

This is brilliant for checking out some of the most famous pictures in the world, including the Mona Lisa, of course. It's not particularly fast, due mainly to the exceptional pictorial content.

www.nationalgallery.org.uk

The National Gallery

Overall rating: ★★★★★			
Classification:	Gallery	**Readability:**	★★★★
Updating:	Monthy	**Reliability:**	★★★★★
Navigation:	★★★★★	**Speed:**	★★★★

UK £ R

A lovely site from the UK's National Gallery, based in London, complete with selected pictures and general information about the gallery. A comprehensive site guide makes navigation easy.

SPECIAL FEATURES

The Collection Details of the National Gallery collection is provided via access to the four main wings of the gallery: the Sainsbury Wing (paintings from 1260-1510), the West Wing (paintings from 1510-1600), the North Wing (paintings from 1600-1700) and the East Wing (paintings from 1700-1900). Each of these four main sites have a selection of the more famous pictures, with details about the painting and its content.

Information gives details about opening times, guided visits for children, cafés, the picture library, location and transport. There is also a floorplan of the National Gallery, useful for planning trips.

What's New includes an art game, plus information about lectures, courses and new publications.

Other features

Make use of the search facility which provides additional information and links outside the National Gallery. Also check out the site for information about future exhibitions.

www.studyweb.com

Study Web

Overall rating: ★★★★★

Classification:	Information	**Readability:**	★★★
Updating:	Regularly	**Reliability:**	★★★★
Navigation:	★★★	**Speed:**	★★★

UK

A UK-based links site aimed at parents, students, teachers and school administrators. It has a wide subject range, providing access to a stated 118,000 sites – so you should be able to find help on any subject. And it's fairly easy to use. For example, to find English National Ballet go to Fine Arts/Dance/Ballet. To locate the Globe Theatre site, go to Fine Arts/Theatre/Shakespearean Theatre. Moving around the site itself is fine although the links are slow.

SPECIAL FEATURES

Homework Help provides an additional range of categorisation to help students find out where to look.

Study Buddy provides online resources such as a dictionary, thesaurus, medical dictionary, measurement converter, maps, US phone directory and CIA world fact book: this is an unexpectedly useful resource!

Links Each URL listed has a short recommendation which gives an idea of the visual content, age range suitable (although this is done with the US system of Grade levels), and a brief description. Plus, via Study Buddy, links to encyclopedia.com and similar.

Visit this site when you need to find information. It is a very useful site for children researching homework, students with projects, and for parents who want to help them access helpful sites.

www.crayola.com

Crayola

Overall rating: ★★★★

Classification:	Information	**Readability:**	★★★
Updating:	Weekly	**Reliability:**	★★★
Navigation:	★★★	**Speed:**	★★★

US

This is the site of the US-based Crayola crayon (and other items) manufacturers. It is a huge site and great fun to explore. Check out Crafts, packed with ideas for things to make, or Stories where you can follow an on-going tale. Note that Macromedia Shockwave needs downloading for some of the options (for example, to print a picture for colouring in), but it can be downloaded free from the site.

SPECIAL FEATURES

Pre-school section where you can print out numbers and letters for colouring in, although unfortunately all the letters are upper case which goes against the standard advice of teaching small children lower case letters first. Also the letter sounds aren't accurate for first phonetics ('S', for example, is for Snowman ('sn' sound), rather than the more phonetically accurate Sun).

Inspiration leads to an Artists' corner, with information about Michelangelo, Leonardo da Vinci and Keith Haring. It could do with more, as this makes an excellent introduction. There is a really good section for teachers, kids and parents on artistic techniques and how to get the best from some of these products. Also in the Inspiration section is Poetry Place. Look here to find a wonderful selection of poets by subjects (such as the Moon, a section which includes poems by WB Yeats, Hilaire Belloc, as well as the traditional Man in the Moon).

Other features

Search Although there is no heavy sell and products and prices are only guaranteed for the US market, there is a good 'selection' search service where you can match age to different products. This provides good ideas for grandparents, those without children, and those not familiar with differently aged children to our own!

There's lots of interest on this site, including a history of Crayola from its origins in 1885. Spelling throughout the text is American, so expect 'color' for colour, and so on. Although downloading the pictures takes a bit of time, it is a site with lots to offer a range of differently aged children, from pre-schoolers to those at secondary school.

www.eduweb.co.uk

Overall rating: ★★★★

Classification:	Information	**Readability:**	★★★
Updating:	Monthly	**Reliability:**	★★★★
Navigation:	★★★	**Speed:**	★★★★

UK £ R

Primarily this is a UK-based internet service designed for teachers and pupils, providing free access to NetPals, (an internet pen-pal service for those aged 5-19), Projects, the At School Directory of educational sites, Staffroom and Discussion groups. Two other sites, Pathways and At School Web publishing, are available on subscription.

SPECIAL FEATURES

NetPals is an international service, and can be an interesting way for children to learn about life in other cultures.

Living Library is a good curriculum resource, itself resourced from an impressive range (from the Corbis Picture Library to the Independent newspaper), but because this site is primarily designed for schools there is a subscription charge which has to be paid before you can access it. For home users there is a special price of £49.99 plus VAT for one year's access, but you have to phone up to subscribe.

Links to other sites via the Pathways option if you are a Living Library subscriber. Plus links to internet search engines such as Yahoo and Alta Vista. You'll also find access to numerous school websites, complete with Eduweb's winner of the week!

Not necessarily a first port of call, but worth checking out if you have school-age children who do endless project work!

www.tate.org.uk

The Tate Galleries

Overall rating: ★★★★

Classification:	Gallery	**Readability:**	★★★★
Updating:	Regularly	**Reliability:**	★★★★★
Navigation:	★★★★	**Speed:**	★★★★

UK

This site serves as a very good introduction to the three Tate Galleries (London, Liverpool and St Ives) and provides a wealth of information about the twentieth-century artists in the collection.

SPECIAL FEATURES

Gallery information provides all you need to know about visiting each gallery, including opening times, restaurant facilities, current and future exhibitions, and details of how to get there.

Collections Around 8,000 works from the Tate Galleries are illustrated online. More will become available over time.

Education sections in each of the gallery sites give details of both regular and special events and how to plan a visit – schools groups currently need to book five months in advance. It is also possible to book regular talks and workshops.

Other features

Online ordering is possible from the Tate Gallery shop, which sells books, postcards, posters and prints. Also visit the Discussion forum where you can post your comments and raise queries (there are quite a lot of requests for help with coursework!).

Details are provided of the new Tate Modern development, due to open in Bankside Power Station in May 2000.

www.funbrain.com

Fun Brain

Overall rating: ★★★

Classification:	Information	**Readability:**	★★★
Updating:	Regularly	**Reliability:**	★★★★
Navigation:	★★★	**Speed:**	★★★★

US

Funbrain.com was developed by a software company in the States who specialise in developing risk management and training systems for banks and option traders. They wanted to apply the same systems to educational games for children which led to this site. It is divided into material for kids in four different age groups, in addition to sections for teachers and parents. You can also select games by topic (such as Culture, Universe, Words, and Numbers).

SPECIAL FEATURES

Four age ranges: 6 and under, 7-10, 11-14, and 15 up, each section packed with games.

Quiz Lab in the Teachers section allows teachers to make quizzes for students to complete online.

Other features

Links to advertisers, and a Search option as a parental resource in the Parents section.

This is a great site with masses on it – although it can be hard, even at the lowest level (it would be a good way of revising for an appearance on 'Who Wants to be a Millionaire'!). But overall, there are a good range of questions for different children's ages and abilities. There is also a Curriculum Guide, but this is for the States and not linked to the UK's National Curriculum.

www.shoo-rayner.co.uk Shoo Rayner			
Overall rating: ★★★			
Classification:	Personal	**Readability:**	★★★
Updating:	Weekly	**Reliability:**	★★★
Navigation:	★★★	**Speed:**	★★★★
UK			

This is the site for the children's book author Shoo Rayner. It provides masses of fun and games for fans of his work, plus introduces it to those not yet in the know. The site also provides 'added value' if you have the books, but this isn't necessary.

SPECIAL FEATURES

Book list of everything published by this author/illustrator, including out-of-print titles

Ideas for teachers provides background suggestions for things to do on the site.

Link to amazon.co.uk for book sales.

www.schools.co.uk Schools Co			
Overall rating: ★★			
Classification:	E-commerce	**Readability:**	★★
Updating:	Monthly	**Reliability:**	★★★
Navigation:	★★	**Speed:**	★★★
UK			

This site is aimed at teachers and librarians and is primarily a book-ordering site. Books are often discounted and available direct from the site or via WHSmith online (to which there is a link).

SPECIAL FEATURES

Parents lists books by subject category. (Note that most of these books are pretty academic in nature.) Parents are invited to apply to review books. They are also launching a site reviewing schools in the same way.

Although it claims to update monthly, in February there were still ' Christmas activities'. Readability is poor because the design makes the site confusing to get around. And it's difficult to get back from the WHSmiths site.

Chapter 7

Shopping

Never has armchair shopping been so easy. If you have reservations about shopping online, becoming a parent may change that as it's so easy. With the right sites it's quick and efficient compared to trailing around a shop trying to find what you want. Many sites now have online ordering using credit card data which is secure and encrypted so it is accessible only by the supplier, making it extremely safe as well as convenient. Not only that, but many sites who have a vested interest in encouraging you to buy, provide lots of suggestions about suitability to age, and ability, which is useful if you don't know or can't remember what five-year old girls are obsessed with. While some sites represent vast department stores, others provide the benefit of small, specialist outlets without all the hassle of physically going to find them. However, in many cases the postage, packing or delivery charge far outweighs the cost of travel or time to purchase something from a shop so look out for hidden extras.

www.urchin.co.uk

Urchin

Overall rating: ★★★★★

Classification:	E-commerce	**Readability:**	★★★★★
Updating:	Regularly	**Reliability:**	★★★★
Navigation:	★★★★★	**Speed:**	★★★★

UK

Urchin is a UK-based mail-order company describing itself as providing 'designs for modern families'. The online catalogue contains around 300 furnishing, furniture and accessory items, including a small range of interesting toys, for babies, toddlers and kids. You can also order the free catalogue to be sent by mail. The design and layout is funky and the whole site is very easy to navigate. You can also register on-line to receive regular e-newsletters and a guest section to air your views.

SPECIAL FEATURES

Go Shopping gives the complete catalogue available to buy online. Each item has a photograph and a detailed description with a reference number and price. The products are all carefully sourced, and are arranged into categories with clever titles as follows:

Feed 'Em Up All you need for the kitchen includes bibs, eating utensils and tumblers.

We've Got Wheels An extensive range of bike and car seats and accessories, and several all terrain pushchairs including rain covers, sun shades, cosy fleeces and accoutrements.

Outdoor Elements A wide selection of outdoor rainwear (jackets, dungarees, hats), picnic rugs, baby carriers and Brio toy buckets and spades.

Holiday Urchin seems to have everything for travelling with babies and young children. This includes a travel sterilizer, Sposh ozone sunsuits to protect from UV rays, hats, towels, sunglasses for the beach as well as swimming accessories (inflatable rings, armbands) and also travel cots and sleeping bags.

Ooooh Baby! Cover cots, cribs, changing bags, mobiles and other baby equipment.

Kid's Rooms Interesting furniture, expensive beds and chairs but also cheaper storage ideas for clothes rails, memo boards, display boards and frames, chairs and beanbags.

Gadgets and Technology Fading lights as well as child-friendly computer equipment such as mouse mats, mini-mouses and CD-ROMS.

Ablutions Lots of fun bath toys, washbags and towels as well as more serious things like First Aid kits and thermometers.

Bold At Bedtime Bedding, blankets, baby sleeping bags, and slippers

Lighten Up A good range of brightly coloured funky lights and shades

It's A Wrap Gift ideas, special treats for dolls and teddies

Bargains, Bargains, Bargains A selection of discounted items available

Massively Discounted Swimwear A seasonal sale area, currently selling off last year's swimwear.

This site comes highly recommended. It has great products to sell, presented in a well-thought-out and attractive design. It is easy to navigate and the descriptions of the products are clear and well-written. Definitely worth a visit, either for shopping for your own home or for presents.

www.boden.co.uk

Boden

Overall rating: ★★★★			
Classification:	E-commerce	**Readability:**	★★★★
Updating:	Regularly	**Reliability:**	★★★★
Navigation:	★★★	**Speed:**	★★★★

UK

Online shopping from the UK-based mail-order outlet Boden, stocks clothes for women, men and children. You can request a free catalogue which makes selecting online easier. It has a good range of upmarket basics which are not cheap, but good quality. They have nice accessories which include hats and shoes, plus French wellies. The site is very easy to navigate either by category or via the search facility, although you need to be quite general in your request. The top left corner of the screen keeps a running total of the amount currently in your shopping trolley. The on-line ordering is secure and delivery should be within 4-5 days of despatch.

SPECIAL FEATURES

Face of Boden is an opportunity for budding models. Send in a full-length photograph of your child and they might be selected to model in a forthcoming Boden catalogue.

Sale shop gives details of dates of sales held at their sale shops in London and both sales items and items specially discounted for online-only sales.

Request a catalogue to be sent to you by mail.

This is a straightforward shopping site with good kids basics as well as a good selection for women and men. It has practical nicely designed clothes which last, catering mainly for the 1-12 age group. Personal text by Johnnie Boden is a nice touch.

www.dawson-and-son.com

Dawson and Son

Overall rating: ★★★★			
Classification:	E-commerce	**Readability:**	★★★★
Updating:	Regularly	**Reliability:**	★★★★
Navigation:	★★★★	**Speed:**	★★★

UK

This is the site for the UK-based mail-order toy catalogue, Dawson and Son, famous for their beautiful, hardwearing toys made from sustainable wood. The online catalogue shows photographs of toys organised into groups such as Young Children, Imaginative Play, Active Play, Educational, Jigsaws, Older Children and Decorative Letters. As well as toys and dolls houses, there are outdoor games such as ride-on scooters, skipping ropes, and croquet sets.

The quality of the merchandise is very high. If you want a really good value dolls' house, plus a range of contents, look no further – a little girl's dream.

There is a secure ordering facility, they will ship worldwide which makes this a good choice for sending childrens toys as gifts to friends abroad. There is also a currency conversion, updated on a daily basis for those buying from abroad.

An easily accessible site which should be on every parent's list whether buying special presents for their own children or presents for others.

www.eToys.co.uk eToys (UK) Ltd			
Overall rating: ★★★★			
Classification:	E-commerce	**Readability:**	★★★★
Updating:	Monthly	**Reliability:**	★★★★
Navigation:	★★★★	**Speed:**	★★★
UK			

This is a leading web-based retailer focusing exclusively on children's products. It is the UK subsidiary of eToys Inc, a publicly owned US-based company. This is an excellent shopping site if a little slow, but well-organised given its extent with easy-to-find categories plus quicksearch option. It is heavily geared towards merchandised toys, though this isn't to the detriment of other products.

There is a secure online ordering with fast delivery – even close to Christmas and a choice of delivery times and costs.

SPECIAL FEATURES:

Search is a very good database searchable by age (from 0-9+ years), by toy brands (including Crayola, Barbie, GALT, LEGO, Tomy), by favourite characters (such as Postman Pat, Noddy, Pokemon, Sindy), and toy categories (for example Action Figures, Arts & Crafts, Dolls, Toddlers & Preschool).

Toy recommendations includes **Bestsellers** as well as the section **Twenty under £20** with a good range of toys sub-divided by age-range, useful for quickly checking-out age-appropriate toys at a reasonable price. Under this heading is also a pick of the month section with a changing selection of toys categorised by age for easy reference.

From the Movies gives an excellent video selection, plus games and software.

Gift services section provides gift wrapping, gift certificates plus that all-important birthday reminder!

My wish list is a registration mechanism where you fill in your details, along with a record of any products that you may want to buy at a later date. The idea is that you then send the list to friends and family, but you do need to open an eToys account to create the list.

Not only is this a good site for parents, but also for grandparents, bachelor uncles, child-free godparents and all those other people who endlessly ask you to suggest something around Christmas or the time of your child's birthday! Failing that, you can ask them to give your child an eToys gift voucher.

www.toyzone.co.uk

Toy Zone

Overall rating: ★★★★

Classification:	E-commerce	**Readability:**	★★★★
Updating:	Weekly	**Reliability:**	★★★★
Navigation:	★★★	**Speed:**	★★★★

UK

This is a heavy-duty, UK-based TV and film or multimedia merchandising site, with not a wax crayon or book to be seen. That said, if you are after the latest Furby, Game Boy product, Lego, Pokemon, Thomas the Tank Engine or Tweenie item, it will probably be easiest to look for it here first. It is easy to navigate with the contents buttons remaining on screen at all times. Online ordering is secure and you can send Toyzone products direct to the recipient – good news for those who leave present shopping to the last minute. This even applies to placing orders if you live outside the UK, as long as the recipient's address is in the UK.

SPECIAL FEATURES

A sophisticated search is available to look for toys in a number of ways, either a keyword search if you know what you want or you can browse by department with a choice of categories as follows:

Hot, hot, hot section with all the current favourites such as Pokemon, Toy Story, Tweenies, Barbie, and Flick Trix

Fast track has a selection of bestsellers, under £20, a deal of the week, collectibles, characters, and key brands

Recommended section is grouped by age (0-3 years, 3-6 years, 6-8 years, 8 plus).

Big kids features Dreamcast, South Park and Lara Croft games.

Wish list section where you can create your own wish list to email to friends and relations

Special offers are updated regularly and contain offers such as price reductions, free product with orders of a certain value, buy two and get one 'three', and so on.

Play option requires Macromedia Flash 4.0 to run which can be downloaded from the site. Choose from Planet Nutty, Planet Snooze, Planet Gloss and Planet Mystery.

As toy sites go this is a good one, largely because you will probably find what you want, as long as it falls within the above criteria.

www.toysrus.co.uk

Toys R Us

Overall rating: ★★★★

Classification:	E-commerce	**Readability:**	★★★★
Updating:	Regularly	**Reliability:**	★★★★
Navigation:	★★★★	**Speed:**	★★★★

UK

This is the UK-based website for the nationwide chain of Toys R Us stores, providing online shopping. It has an extensive range, from toddler toys to multimedia PCs, go-karts to video games, and fashion dolls to board games. It probably helps to know roughly what you want before you start because there are no recommended sections (such as those which are so useful on other sites with similar extensive ranges). It is arranged like an online catalogue with categories which makes access to the ranges very easy, plus there are Department search and Toy search options on the Home page. The Home Delivery button allows you to check on the progress of your order at any stage. Toys R Us have also linked up with breathe.net to allow Free Internet Access either by ordering a CD or signing up directly online.

SPECIAL FEATURES

Online catalogue shows the categories of toys available and makes finding your way round easy.

Encyclopedia section gives links to several leading toy maker websites.

Current Adverts is an area to check out special promotions for money-off offers and savings.

Gold Card section lets you apply for a loyalty card so you earn points for purchases, then you receive money-off coupons. For example, if you spend between £100 and £199.99 you receive £50 in coupons, and if you spend £500 or more, you receive £150 in coupons.

Mobile Phone Deals is a link through to direct sales of mobile phones which doesn't necessarily seem to fit with toy sales.

Links direct to babiesrus.co.uk and to leading toymaker sites such as Hornby, Scalextric, Tomy and Mattel.

ToysRus is not dissimilar from the other large toy sites, concentrating primarily on mainstream toys, but prices are competitive and home delivery is priced at a very reasonable £2.50 per order.

www.babiesrus.co.uk

Babies R Us

Overall rating: ★★★

Classification:	E-commerce	**Readability:**	★★★★
Updating:	Regularly	**Reliability:**	★★★
Navigation:	★★★	**Speed:**	★★★

UK

Billed as 'Everything you need for your new arrival' this is the UK-based site for the Babies R Us chain, with its 63 stores nationwide. It is a subsidiary of its parent store, Toys R Us, and benefits from the marketing and sales expertise gleaned from the earlier existence of the initial store. You can choose from over 800 products, buy online with a secure order facility, and have them delivered to your door. Everything is grouped into categories with advice and information as well as shopping. There is a link back to Toys R Us.

SPECIAL FEATURES

Baby Advice Although product-led, this can be useful when trying to assess, for example, how long a moses basket will last your newborn baby. It also includes subject-led information; for example, in the bedtime section there is an article about reducing the risk of cot death. However, although the information provided is good, this section is limited and could easily be improved upon.

On the Move contains a good selection of relevant products such as car seats, carriers, pushchairs, travel sets and travelling on holiday.

At Home includes advice on kitting out the nursery, products for bathtime, bedtime, cots, baskets, highchairs as well as other large baby equipment.

Everyday Essentials covers the important areas of books, feeding, home safety, hygiene and nappies.

Just for Fun gives playtime products.

The straightforward shopping online is to be commended, but the baby advice section could be greatly improved upon for the benefit of new and prospective parents. An obvious addition would be a useful links section – not to other stores, but to helpful organisations for new parents.

www.boots.co.uk

Boots Co

Overall rating: ★★★

Classification:	E-commerce	**Readability:**	★★★★
Updating:	Monthly	**Reliability:**	★★★★
Navigation:	★★★★	**Speed:**	★★★★

UK

This is the on-line shopping arm of the Boots high street store with its extensive range. There are no links to other sites which is a bit of a missed opportunity.

SPECIAL FEATURES

Mother and Baby covers everything for the pregnant mother-to-be, for the newborn up to toddler age group. It has everything from cotton wool buds to pushchairs.

Boots Consultant has features about looking after your complexion. You choose from a pull-down menu the products you need and the action you should take. How you feel today, in a party mood, I've got PMT, I want a treat, I feel flu-ey, to get advice. There is also a section to fill in details to find your skin type although I expect that anyone getting this far probably knows this already.

Index takes you straight to a health, beauty and parenting health section where you can browse easily accessible topics. Choose from contraception and fertility, pregnancy, mother and baby, alternative health, the teenage years, dental health, and more. There is also a search option.

Community forum option You need to register to use this section which has lots of discussion topics. However, this isn't yet a busy part of the site and lots of the postings are quite old.

Online magazine contains features with a women's health and beauty emphasis, not specifically aimed at parents,but then sometimes you need to think of yourself as well. This month they are on subjects such as Dyeing for a change – do blondes have more fun? Down to earth – natural beauty products; Welcome to the Pleasure Dome gives detailed features about the Millenium Dome (the Body Zone is sponsored by Boots) as well as an archive of past features.

The primary advantage of this site is to shop online, with its benefits of easy access to the well-known high-street brand Boots products. While the Boots catalogue includes good information, this site is a little patchy, with some areas of information better than others.

www.hamleys.co.uk

Hamleys

Overall rating: ★★★

Classification:	E-commerce	**Readability:**	★★★★
Updating:	Monthly	**Reliability:**	★★★★
Navigation:	★★★	**Speed:**	★★★★

UK

The website of the 'most famous toy shop in the world' according to its blurb. It is a UK-based site which caters for shoppers both in the UK and also Europe, America and Canada – which makes it very easy, for example, to buy an authentic Paddington Bear for an American relative. There is a good range of toy items, including special exclusive Hamley's toys (such as customised toy taxis and London buses or the Hamley's Humpty Dumpty). The shopping area is arranged in three main sections: by categories (collectables, cuddly toys, dolls, exclusives, games & puzzles, something different), by recommendations (Hamley's top five at any one time – and also by filling in the sex, age and price range you are interested in – you get some recommendations) and by age groups.

SPECIAL FEATURES

Interactive kids club gives instructions on sending an e-card, games to play on line, pictures to be printed out and coloured in and a monthly top five recommended toys category.

Currency option Option to view prices and to pay in either sterling or dollars (essential if outside the European union).

This is a nice looking site aiming to enhance the Hamley's brand and to sell toys. The exclusive category and the Hamley's recommendations are for non-merchandised toys such as collectable teddys rather than Barbies. The prices are not cheap but good for buying presents when something special is required.

www.trotters.co.uk

Trotters

Overall rating: ★★★

Classification:	E-commerce	**Readability:**	★★★★
Updating:	Regularly	**Reliability:**	★★★★
Navigation:	★★★	**Speed:**	★★★★

UK

Trotters originated as a one-stop children's shop in London, catering for 0-10 year olds, complete with hairdressers, clothes, shoes, books, toys and a juice bar. There are now two shops in London, a mail order service and this online shopping facility of a selected rangeof clothes. The range includes designer brands from Paul Smith, DKNY, Kenzo, Timberland and Quiksilver.

SPECIAL FEATURES

Trotters Direct Online shopping from the catalogue which you can order to be sent to you, or order directly on-line. They have a good range of upmarket children's clothes divided into categories such as t-shirts, other tops, trousers, shorts, outerwear, sleepy wear, swimwear, underwear, footwear and baby clothes.

In the Beginning gives a history of the shops, set up in 1990 by Sophie Mirman and Richard Ross, the husband and wife team responsible for Tie Rack and Sock Shop.

This is a good straightforward, small website for on-line shopping of a range of good quality, although pricey children's clothes. Shopping online takes the Trotters range to a further, although not a primary, audience.

www.mothercare.co.uk

Mothercare

Overall rating: ★★

Classification:	E-commerce	**Readability:**	★★★★
Updating:	Regularly	**Reliability:**	★★★★
Navigation:	★★★	**Speed:**	★★★

UK

Online shopping from the UK-based chain of specialist mother and baby shops. The site is not particularly easy to find your way around as it is difficult to get back to the home page. There is online shopping from over 2,000 items, but you need a copy of the catalogue from which to order as items are not available to view on the site. You can order the free catalogue online or by telephone from the customer care line (open Monday to Friday, 9 am to 5 pm).

A useful pregnancy advice leaflet which is available in-store, is also available on the website with Adobe Acrobat Reader (which can be downloaded free).

Other than its role as an online shopping site, there isn't currently much else to recommend this site. There are details of the new in-store Mothercare magazine, priced £2.00, which probably has lots of interesting information for parents and mums-to-be – so maybe the lack of site material will be addressed in the near future.

www.elc.co.uk

Early Learning Centre

Overall rating: ★★

Classification:	E-commerce	**Readability:**	★★★★
Updating:	Regularly	**Reliability:**	★★★★
Navigation:	★★	**Speed:**	★★★★

UK

A site from the UK-based Early Learning Centre, which has 217 stores throughout the UK and a mail order service already in operation. Those familiar with the shop will find the site easy to use and therefore easy to shop from, those who are new to it may need to spend more time browsing.

SPECIAL FEATURES

Browse the Shop this is the best way to explore the site and it is sub-divided by category and age-range. Alternatively, you can go direct to the online shopping section, especially if you are familiar with the Early Learning Centre products and their mail-order catalogue.

Playtime section with dot-to-dot pictures which can be printed off, an animal sound recognition game (needs Macromedia Shockwave, which can be downloaded from the site), missing letters game, and others – although this could provide much more, and could be a real feature of the site by linking to sites of the suggested products.

Links To the NSPCC site (worth a look at www.nspcc.org.uk) and also the John Menzies Group, ELC's parent company.

The site is probably of most use for dedicated ELC shoppers – those who already know how good the stores are, and know the range of products – but for the new ELC customer, this is a site worth developing further. One obvious section is to include information about how children learn, the importance of play, and what parents can do to facilitate this, tied in with product recommendations. The Playtime section could be developed further, with lower case alphabet letters that could be printed out and coloured in, for example. At present however, apart from the shopping facility, this site is a bit of a missed opportunity.

ALSO WORTH MENTIONING

www.clothworks.co.uk
A catalogue of products. Ordering facility not yet available online, but coming shortly.

www.greenfibres.com
Eco-goods and eco-garments for women, men, children and babies available soon online.

Chapter 8

Holidays and Activities

Keeping children happy and occupied is one of the great unsung tasks of parenthood. Finding safe, gainful occupations for older children and teens is becoming increasingly easy and now there is access to a number of specialist organisations, with a wealth of experience and expertise to consider, via the internet. Not only that, but there is greater recognition of the desire for many families to find activities to do together, and a number of sites are providing scope for travel, for example, which promotes just that. In addition, a site like the Foreign Office's also include useful links to other organisation of value when it comes to travel.

www.campbeaumont.com Camp Beaumont			
Overall rating: ★★★★★			
Classification:	Organisation	**Readability:**	★★★★
Updating:	Regularly	**Reliability:**	★★★★
Navigation:	★★★★	**Speed:**	★★★★
UK			

This is the website for the UK-based holiday activities company, providing all details of their day and residential camps for children aged between three and 15 years old. With over 20 years experience, the camps provide welcome holiday care and respite for harassed parents - and there's something for most kids to enjoy. The website is very clearly laid out, not extensive but with all the information you might need if you were interested in holiday activities for your children. Brightly coloured buttons across the top of the page lead to the seven main areas of the site.

SPECIAL FEATURES

Our Camps gives details of the camps for this year. There are four residential camps, including one in France. Some residential camps also include a 4-day or 3-day stay option, which could be ideal for children just starting to spend time at camps and who are insecure about a longer stay at first. There are eight day camps in and around the London area and transport, at an additional cost, is also possible from pick-up points in the area. Prices for each camp are quoted in each section.

Programmes gives details of the wide range of programmes available. These are first divided into Language Programmes featuring English language teaching for three hours each day, for overseas students visiting the residential camps and this gives plenty of information about excursions to local places of interest as well as details about food, sleeping arrangments, safety and medical problems. . There are also Activity Programmes for English speaking children, depending upon whether you are at a residential or day camp. Details are given of the age-appropriate activities for different groups: ages 3-4; 5-7; 8-11; and 12-15. In addition there is a section for the Special Interest activities which are at an additional cost and include Tennis Academy (8-15 year olds); Motorsports (8-15 year olds); Watersports (5-7 year olds), Big Top Circus School, Football Camp, Futurecamp (technology), Horse Riding, Stage & Screen (acting camp).

Parent Guide Information section on safety, healthcare, staff, which are obviously of a very high standard and makes you feel comfortable about sending your child off to camp.

Online Booking is possible but it seems to cater more for the residential camps than the day camps.

Bulletin Board makes interesting reading, and provides some insight for novice campers, sub-divided into campers, parents and staff sections.

Camp Souvenirs is currently under construction but I imagine will sell online the merchandise currently available in their brochure such as baseball caps, t-shirts.

Brochure enquiry you fill in a form and email it to request a brochure.

This is a basic, but clear and non-commercial website explaining what Camp Beaumont is, definitely worth a look if you are looking for summer holiday activities for your children.

www.family-travel.co.uk

Family Travel Magazine

Overall rating: ★★★★			
Classification:	Personal	**Readability:**	★★★★
Updating:	Quarterly	**Reliability:**	★★★★
Navigation:	★★★★	**Speed:**	★★★★

UK

This is the website for the UK-based quarterly, subscription magazine Family Travel, so it is primarily an advertisement for this product which is not available yet online. However it gives a comprehensive overview of this privately produced magazine. It gives details of how to subscribe to the magazine, and you can order back issues of interest. Kate Calvert, the editor, is a very experienced travel writer and mother and it shows, the level of detail of information is fantastic and of enormous value to parents taking children on holiday. The website takes no advertising so the advice is unbiased and features are selected by request from readers.

SPECIAL FEATURES

What we provide gives details of frequently asked questions that the author provides in the magazine such as are cots/high chairs available? Can kids eat in the restaurant? What is there to do with kids?

About the Publication tells you about the editor, Kate Calvert who has been a travel writer for 12 years and now takes her daughter on frequent trips. This section explains the whole philosophy of the magazine and the website which is no pictures, just plain practical information and lots of it!

Taster report gives an example of a report from the magazine. It provides exceptionally useful information about the Vaucluse of southern France, and a good indication of what to expect from the magazine itself. Information is given about places to stay, attitudes to children and babies in general, places to go, when to go, getting there and getting around once you're there. There is also details of several hotels and B & Bs (Chambres d'hote) as well as a brief history of the area, and details of museums, animals and other activities.

Useful Sites is a directory of links to other sites. One of the best aspects of this site are the extensive links whether you want the World Heritage List or the English Tourist Board, travel guides (Rough Guides, Lonely Planet, Michelin, etc.) to worldwide maps, cheap flights to money guides.

This website could still benefit from some development, being able to subscribe to the magazine online for instance, but for new and old parents, who want to get the best out of travelling with their children, this is an excellent resource.

www.pgl.co.uk

PGL

Overall rating: ★★★★

Classification:	Organisation	**Readability:**	★★★★
Updating:	Regularly	**Reliability:**	★★★★
Navigation:	★★★★	**Speed:**	★★★★

UK

This is the UK-based site for PGL Travel, activity holiday specialists for young people aged 6 to 18 years old. All activities take place in a 'safe but challenging environment where children and teenagers with no previous experience can explore their potential, discover hidden talents, learn new skills, and gain self-confidence...' which says it all, really. There are twenty-three PGL centres, with 15 in the UK and eight in France and over 60 activities are available including pony-trekking, abseiling, sailing, archery, etc. PGL instructors have experience and qualifications in their specific area, but they also receive training and monitoring throughout their employment with PGL. There is also organised rail and coach travel, with travel couriers, available.

The site is divided into three main categories with specific names listed down the left side of the page at all times so it is very easy to find your way around.

SPECIAL FEATURES

School/Group Tours and Courses gives details of a variety of adventure trips: PGL Adventure UK are a list of residential group/school centres, 13 in the UK. These have outdoor courses with a wide choice of activities and are also great for improving personal and social skills. PGL Adventure France and Spain gives details of similar courses in Europe. Other features are PGL Exploring Information Technology, PGL Ski Europe which is school ski trips by coach or plane to Austria, France, Italy or Switzerland as well as an American ski programme in New Hampshire. PGL Mission Earth is environmental education combined with outdoor activities aimed at primary school children. Finally, PGL Loch Ranza on the Isle of Arran is a purpose built field studies centre. However, detailed information is not available online, you have to request a brochure.

Seasonal Employment and Training Opportunities for those aged 18 plus. The website gives details of positions vacant and their locations plus what they can offer you as well as training and qualifications both given and required.

Other features

This includes a bulletin board, which can be accessed without registration in order to look at entries, postcards to email to your friends, and a site map as well a brochure request online.

Links to other sites includes a great selection to all sorts of bodies to do with sporting and leisure activities (for example to organisations for fencing, canoeing, skiing, yachting and windsurfing), educational links (such as the BBC and Channel 4 websites as well as directories of educational links) and a mixed bag of general interest links.

The site acts to give you an overview of PGL and what is can do for you. However it would benefit from providing costs and online booking to make it really useful. Instead, you can make a provisional booking only. What is probably most advantageous is to have requested the brochure first, which provides much more comprehensive information, before making a selection.

www.families.co.uk

Families

Overall rating: ★★★			
Classification:	Organisation	**Readability:**	★★★
Updating:	Sometimes	**Reliability:**	★★★
Navigation:	★★★	**Speed:**	★★★

UK

The site opens with a bright yellow background to the home page, certainly noticeable but probably not great if you've been surfing extensively and have tired eyes! There is very little in the way of introduction to this website, really a list of topics down the left side of the page. These vary enormously in the amount of information they provide. For instance books, play equipment, u.v. clothing just lead to a single link site selling one relevant article. Other topics offer more, although Play Areas and Party Venues has a searchable database but only came up with one in Greater London!

SPECIAL FEATURES

Holidays gives details of top 10 resorts, tour operators and a searchable (but not extensive) holiday finder for a seasonal suggested holiday, currently showing ski-ing holidays.

Family history is one of the most extensive areas giving detailed information about genealogy and how to start searching for your family history. The authors are obviously very keen on this as the feature ends with 'There is no cure for the Genealogy bug'!

Where to go gives a list of Uk places of interest to visit, Hotels gives a good list - nine around the UK, which are deemed to be child-friendly, but only one sentence about each one.

This has an interesting variety of links to other sites, from the independent schools site to exchange and mart, which make it worth checking out.

Activities and leisure opportunities - from books to football training for kids in France - are covered on this UK-based site. It is not particularly extensive, and sometimes a little idiosyncratic in its choices, but there are some good items which make it worth a quick look.

www.baha.org.uk

British Activity Holiday Association

Overall rating: ★★★

Classification:	Organisation	**Readability:**	★★★★
Updating:	**Regularly**	**Reliability:**	★★★★
Navigation:	★★★	**Speed:**	★★★

UK

This is the official site for the UK-based British Activity Holiday Association and as such, a first port of call for access to its members. It is divided into five sections with a 'star' button with the initial letter on, to each, as follows: Adults, Children, Families, Groups, Schools, Management Training. Within each of these categories is a list (and links through to) of the private sector centres catering for each group. Beside the name of each place is a grid showing stars illustrating the other groups the centre is suitable for. In all it lists 23 private sector activity organisations for children, families and schools (and adults, groups and management training), of which 15 are geared towards children. All BAHA members have agreed to abide by a code of practice and submit their centres to independent inspection.

There are links to all 23 organisations listed.

This is a listing really of all the members of the association, probably a good way to start looking for an activity holiday, or to check out one you already know about.

www.fco.gov.uk/travel

Foreign Office Travel Advice

Overall rating: ★★★

Classification:	Government	**Readability:**	★★★★
Updating:	Daily	**Reliability:**	★★★★
Navigation:	★★★★	**Speed:**	★★★★

UK

This is the website for the UK's Foreign and Commonwealth Office Travel Advice Unit. The Unit produces a range of information for those travelling abroad and is especially useful for those intending to travel outside the usual holiday destinations. The site has some relevant travel advice for families but there is also a huge amount of information about Foreign Office news and minister's worldwide trips on their daily bulletin.

SPECIAL FEATURES

Travel Advice on major travel destinations is included in a helpful Do's and Don'ts' section. Advice includes specific information on, for example, drugs - ie. death penalty for second offences in India a possibility - while also including advice on medical insurance, motoring offences, and the like which can be very specific to a destination. Each place listed also includes contact phone numbers for a consular officer, in case of emergency. There is also a comprehensive listing of those places in the world not currently recommended for visiting. At all!

There are extensive, but quite quirky, links to other websites, for example leading to all the British Diplomatic Missions, but also to NATO, to the United Nations, to the BBC World Service, the Houses of Parliament, and the UK Passport Agency. What would be useful would be links to anywhere for which you need a visa, and how to go about getting one, but sadly visa information for travelling abroad isn't currently available here.

Not only is this a useful site for those checking out details for family travel, but also for parents whose older children are threatening to travel the world without first checking out their destinations - and some of the problems which could arise.

www.fsc.org.uk

Forest School Camps

Overall rating: ★★

Classification:	Organisation	**Readability:**	★★★
Updating:	Erratically	**Reliability:**	★★
Navigation:	★★★	**Speed:**	★★

UK

This is the UK-based site for Forest School Camps, which originated in the 1930s. Forest School drew its philosophy from progressive education, the Woodcraft movement and the Quakers. They began in 1948, aiming to teach children independence, responsibility, resourcefulness, self-confidence, tolerance and respect. The site lists annual camps and contacts, but you will have to write a letter requesting a brochure.

SPECIAL FEATURES

Programme 2000 gives a list of around 50 camps with details of where the camps are, names of the leaders, age of children they are suitable for, dates of running the camps, and prices.

FSC Reference gives details on information such as How to Enrol, Children with Special Needs, About the Camps, Preparing for the Camps, Lyrics to the Songs.

Other Features.

A Picture Gallery with photographs of children at the camps, Glee is an index of songs which can be download as MP3 files and Latest News which was last updated four months ago!

Links are to sites which are related in philosophy and activity, ie. the Woodcraft Folk, Project HappyChild, Ernest Thompson Seton Institute, etc.

This is a low-tech website which could be capable of much more.

Chapter 9

Miscellany

Financial Planning

There is no doubt children cost money, and numerous banks, building societies and financial planners will outline how much, but education in particular can demand an enormous financial outlay. Planning from birth, and beginning an easy savings plan, can help ease private school fees, extra tuition costs, and university fees later. Many independent financial planners can advise you on what might be worth considering, but these two online services might be worth a look.

www.babybond.co.uk

Tunbridge Wells Equitable Friendly Society

Overall rating: ★★★

Classification:	E-commerce	**Readability:**	★★★
Updating:	Regularly	**Reliability:**	★★★★
Navigation:	★★★★	**Speed:**	★★★

UK

This is the website of the Tunbridge Wells Equitable Friendly Society, focusing on the Baby Bond which is designed to provide you with a tax-exempt savings plan based on a maximum saving per child of £25 a month. It is aimed obviously at selling this financial service and therefore is aimed not only at parents but also at grandparents or generous godparents looking for an investment for the future. It also provides information of other services offered by the financial services company.

There is a Q & A area with answers to several frequently queries that you might have such as how much money to invest? How old should the child be? Who has control?

SPECIAL FEATURES

Calculator button provides a one-click calculation of return on savings so you can calculate how much your child might get back at the end of the policy term.

There is a good selection of links ranging from pregnancy, to parenting, to general, to products and services.

This would be a good starting point for anyone interested in investing for their child's future but you would have to contact them to find out more.

www.ftyourmoney.com Financial Times			
Overall rating: ★★★★			
Classification:	E-commerce	**Readability:**	★★★★
Updating:	Regularly	**Reliability:**	★★★★
Navigation:	★★★★	**Speed:**	★★★★
UK R			

This is an extensive site, from the Financial Times newspaper group, offering a full range of personal finance advice. It also provides a 'News Room' from which you can access up-to-date financial analysis, plus features, covering new products, stock market news, and a problems solved option. Once registered, you also have the options to receive regular news reports in 17 categories, from insurance to tax, pensions to product news.

SPECIAL FEATURES

Your Life Education is divided into six sections:

Pre-school with costs of pre-school education cost including childcare and private nurseries,

Primary & Secondary gives a chart where you fill in the year your child would start and finish private education to calculate the total cost. It gives tips on how to cut the cost of this and also advice on 'hidden' costs even when your child attends state education, for example you might need to buy a more expensive house to live near your chosen, good school, as well as a warning that although your child's basic information might be free there are often outside costs such as extra music, sport and dance lessons.

University section provides monetary advice and budgeting tips for students. Information from the National Union of Students about the true cost of university education suggests that currently the estimated cost of being a student in London costs around £8,000 per 38 week academic year, and nearly £6,000 outside London, this might be a good option to check out! It also gives tips on saving money for students, and a feature on student bank accounts.

Total Cost gives the final total if you have filled in the forms in each of the previous sections.

Paying the Bill gives advice on investing for education and **Investing for Education** outlines the options, which enables you to move towards an individual **My Education Plan.**

There are links to companies to invest in, fund performances, primary private schools and secondary private schools.

This is a comprehensive, personal finance site from the Financial Times Limited, with a good Education section, well worth a visit if you are thinking about planning and investing now for your child's education.

After school

Your child is leaving school and is hoping for a deferred place at university or college. Apart from earning some money in preparation for the student years to come, this can be a time to fulfil one's dreams, to travel the world and to see a bit of life before getting back to academic work. These two sites are very different, the first one is an excellent website to enable parents and teenagers to plan this 'gap year' and to make the most of it. We have also included VSO as it is an excellent website for those considering voluntary work abroad before going on to higher education.

www.gapyear.com

Gap Year

Overall rating: ★★★★

Classification:	Information	**Readability:**	★★★★
Updating:	Regularly	**Reliability:**	★★★★
Navigation:	★★★★	**Speed:**	★★★★

UK £ R

This wonderful site was set up and is run by Tom Griffiths and Richard Knight, both 24, who bring a wealth of experience of use to those planning their gap years – and to their anxious parents!

SPECIAL FEATURES

Gap year opportunities comes with a search facility to find ideas/organisations for gap year projects – from volunteering or teaching to work experience or travel opportunities.

Money matters covers health and insurance, and visas and embassies are all covered.

Message board An active section with lots of messages posted each day. It provides masses of useful information and contacts in itself, whether you want to find out about living in Vietnam, working on a vineyard, securing sponsorship for trips, how to get a visa form from the Indian High Commission, teaching in the Indian Himalayas or details of helpful organisations such as Project Trust. And there's lots of useful feedback from those who have some experience of gap years.

Links to those organisations listed in the Gap Year Opportunities section that have sites.

The reports, diaries, ongoing emails and features written by those currently on their gap years that you' ll find here make the site both useful and fascinating to visit...literally the definitive word(s) on the subject. All-in-all it makes you quite wish you were 18 again, although some of the organisations are not restricted to students...

www.vso.org.uk

Voluntary Service Overseas

Overall rating: ★★★★

Classification:	Charity	**Readability:**	★★★★
Updating:	Regularly	**Reliability:**	★★★★
Navigation:	★★★★	**Speed:**	★★★★

UK £ R

This is the web site of VSO, which sends aid to developing countries in human form. It is a very straightforward site which provides clear information on what VSO does and how to apply. Visit the home page and there is a description of what VSO is.

SPECIAL FEATURE

Explore the world gives fascinating descriptions of what is happening in various parts of the world. The country profiles are a new feature which give a good overview of the political situation in a large number of developing countries as well as describing the VSO programme. Click on one country of your choice and read what is happening there, the nature of the VSO programme and comments from volunteers and from their employers who have worked there.

How to volunteer (with a detailed application form which can be emailed or printed off and posted), campaigns and events which VSO is taking part in, how you can support the work of VSO and publications associated with the charity.

The volunteer! Students and people of different ages who have taken part in VSO over many years.

Safe Surfing

Many parents are concerned about what sort of information their children might access from the web, as well as what personal information they might release. While Pokemon cheats are OK, details of bomb-making, pictures of dead bodies and live pornography aren't, but these are all easy enough to access by a nimble-fingered child. While blocking and censoring programmes do exist, I have it on good authority from one 14-year old that there are ways to get round them, so be warned: they are not foolproof. And it is notoriously easy to access the odd site inadvertently. In a way, perhaps, the best way to use the internet is with the kids, so it becomes a family resource, not a babysitting alternative to the TV when you are desperate for five minutes peace!

Parental common sense should also prevail. Remember to make sure that your child knows not to give out a full name and address, e-mail is Ok as it doesn't give away your whereabouts, but another 'user name' is a good idea. You can also set up some filtering in your web browser by finding your way into the Content Advisor (through content, via internet options in your tools menu) in Internet Explorer.

For more information about safe sites try www.cyberangels.org, which recommends a number of safe search engines including Yahooligans, My.Lycos, and Surfmonkey.com. Other sites which lead to child-friendly sites are www.surfnetkids.com, www.launchsite.org and www.KZuk.net.

www.cyberangels.org

Cyberangels

Overall rating: ★★★★

Classification:	Information	**Readability:**	★★★★
Updating:	Regularly	**Reliability:**	★★★★
Navigation:	★★★★	**Speed:**	★★★★

UK £ R

This is an absolutely straightforward site which offers practical help and guidance on how to protect your children in cyberspace and it is fronted by an American lawyer. The Home Page consists of a series of headings.

SPECIAL FEATURES

Kids Safety on Line, Cyberangels Help, Cyberstalking, Support

You can join the CyberAngels Team (although this is a US site) and you can report any child pornography sites you discover from all over the world.

The best part of the site provides guides on how to guard against children being exploited on and off line. It gives a list of what makes children vulnerable and how to ensure your child is safe. This may sound gloomy, but it is becoming a bigger problem every day in the UK.

ALSO WORTH MENTIONING

Lycos

www.lycos.com and www.lycos.co.uk

The search engine, Lycos, has been at the forefront of making sure that children who surf are safe. Click through to their US site and at the top of the home page you will find **parental controls.** Click through to **Search Guard** which will screen out adult, violent or pornographic sites.

The **LycosZone** (entertainment for kids) is there to keep your children happy.

For those surfers based in the UK, go to www.lycos.co.uk. Look at the home page and click on **Safe search** which can provide links to leading companies who make 'filtering software' which you can download at a special price. Not as advanced or as helpful as their US partners, we would recommend going direct to the US website.

www.Kzuk.net

This is a free ISP for children aged between 4-12. It provides interactives games and activities for children. If you call up their website you can send off for their CD which will screen out undesirable sites and provide loads of entertainment for children.

Also available as free downloads are products from sites such as www.cyberpatrol.co.uk, www.surfwatch.com and www.cybersitter.com.

Buying books and software online

Many of the websites featured in this book, which recommend books also recommend buying them online through www.amazon.co.uk. Amazon was one of the first, and is certainly one of the best online booksellers with extensive stock, good discounts and fast service. Other online book ordering facilities are also available, including sites such as www.bol.com, www.alphabetstreet.com, www.bookpages.com and www.bookshop.co.uk.

You can also access a number of major bookselling chains via the net, including sites such as www.blackwells.co.uk, www.dillons.co.uk, Hammicks at www.thebookplace.com and www.waterstones.co.uk.

Numerous software publishers are also now online, among them are www.europress.co.uk, which offers a wide range of education and reference software for all pre-school, primary, and secondary levels as well as adult products for which you can shop online. www.gspltd.co.uk, also has an extensive range, including the Letts GCSE revision guides.

There are several sites to choose from and they offer a welcome alternative for parents who do not live near or cannot get to a good children's bookshop.

Educational Software

www.learningstore.co.uk
The Learning Store

Overall rating: ★★★★

Classification:	Ecommerce	**Readability:**	★★★★
Updating:	Daily	**Reliability:**	★★★
Navigation:	★★★★	**Speed:**	★★★

UK

Learningstore is a secure shopping web site with over 1000 items of educational software for your home pc and Mac. There are 40 categories of software to choose from including the obvious ones such as those relating to SATs, GCSEs and A levels. There is also loads of software linked to childrens' characters which will teach and entertain at the same time.The home page includes special offers both for action games and GSCE titles, bestsellers and resources. The software is despatched and delivered the next day. Some software is available for mac users.

SPECIAL FEATURES

Learning links provide links to a host of interesting web sites.

Gift ideas A range of products with atttractive discounts.

For schools The learning store provides titles with licences for schools

Advanced search You can specify the age, subject area, publisher or title to find software.

Books

www.amazon.co.uk Amazon			
Overall rating: ★★★★★			
Classification:	Ecommerce	**Readability:**	★★★★
Updating:	Hourly	**Reliability:**	★★★★
Navigation:	★★★★	**Speed:**	★★★★★
UK R			

Amazon have established a big reputation as on line booksellers. It is hard not to be impressed. The site is clear, easy to navigate and updated hourly.

You can go straight from the home page where you choose **Books.** On the books homepage choose **Children's** from the **Browse** section.

SPECIAL FEATURES

On the children's page Amazon offer a range of bestsellers at good discounts. Features include **What we're Reading, Extracts from Novels, Interviews with Authors,** and **What Customers Recommend.**

Children's Essential bookshelf lists books by particular authors, so that if a child discovers an author they like they can choose more by the same person, a great way to encourage more reading.

ALSO WORTH MENTIONING

Ottakars

www.ottakars.co.uk

Ottakars are a chain of high street booksellers with over 70 branches. Their on line bookshop is bright, well designed and easy to navigate. Ottakars promote a range of bestsellers, some at a discount. There are 14 categories of childrens books to browse. The **Author Search** works fast and, for example, listed 300 plus titles under Milne.

From the homepage select category **Browse** and go straight to the **Children's Pages.** On the homepage you can also **Ask the Expert** who will recommend titles for children (and adults!) Ottakars charge postage or will deliver free to your local Ottakars store.

Waterstones

www. waterstones.co.uk

Waterstones has recently redesigned its website. From the homepage you can click on **Children's** and you go straight to the children's section. A children's book of the month is included on the homepage (at a discount).

There are long descriptions of the featured children's books and a dozen categories of children's books to choose from. As with Ottakar's there is an efficient **Author Search** and a recommendation service **Ask a Bookseller.**

My Waterstone's offers registration, express check out and the ability to build a library of favourite titles.

Glossary of Internet Terms

A

Accelerators Add-on programs, which speed up browsing.

Acceptable Use Policy These are the terms and conditions of using the internet. They are usually set by organisations, who wish to regulate an individual's use of the internet. For example, an employer might issue a ruling on the type of email which can be sent from an office.

Access Provider A company which provides access to the internet, usually via a dial-up account. Many companies such as AOL and Dircon charge for this service, although there are an increasing number of free services such as Freeserve, Lineone and Tesco.net. Also known as an Internet Service Provider.

Account A user's internet connection, with an Access/ Internet Service Provider, which usually has to be paid for.

Acrobat Reader Small freely-available program, or web browser plug-in, which lets you view a Portable Document Format (PDF) file.

Across Lite Plug-in which allows you to complete crossword puzzles online.

Address Location name for email or internet site, which is the online equivalent of a postal address. It is usually composed of a unique series of words and punctuation, such as *my.name@myhouse.co.uk*. See also URL.

America Online (AOL) World's most heavily subscribed online service provider.

Animated GIF Low-grade animation technique used on websites.

ASCII Stands for American Standard Code for Information Interchange, It is a coding standard which all computers can recognise, and ensures that if a character is entered on one part of the internet, the same character will be seen elsewhere.

ASCII Art Art made of letters and other symbols. Because it is made up of simple text, it can be recognised by different computers.

ASDL Stands for Asynchronous Digital Subscriber Line, which is a high speed copper wire which will allow rapid transfer of information. Not widely in use at moment, though the government is pushing for its early introduction.

Attachment A file included with an email, which may be composed of text, graphics and sound. Attachments are encoded for transfer across the internet, and can be viewed in their original form by the recipient. An attachment is the equivalent of putting a photograph with a letter in the post.

B

Bookmark A function of the Netscape Netvigator browser which allows you to save a link to your favourite web pages, so that you can return straight there at a later date, without having to re-enter the address. Favourites in internet Explorer is the same thing.

BPS Abbreviation of Bits Per Second, which is a measure of the speed at which information is transferred or downloaded.

Browse Common term for looking around the web. See also Surfing.

Browser A generic term for the software that allows users to move and look around the Web. Netscape Navigator and

Internet Explorer are the ones that most people are familiar with, and they account for 97 percent of web hits.

Bulletin Board Service A BBS is a computer with a telephone connection, which allows you direct contact to upload and download information and converse with other users, via the computer. It was the forerunner to the online services and virtual communities of today.

C

Cache A temporary storage space on the hard drive of your computer, which stores downloaded websites. When you return to a website, information is retrieved from the cache and displayed much more rapidly. However, this information may not be the most recent version for sites which are frequently updated and you will need to reload the Website address for these.

Chat Talking to other users on the web in real time, but with typed, instead of spoken words. Special software such as ICQ or MIRC is required before you can chat.

Chat Room An internet channel which allows several people to type in their messages, and talk to one another over the internet.

Clickstream The trail left as you 'click' your way around the web.

Content The material on a website that actually relates to the site, and is hopefully of interest or value. Things like adverts are not considered to be part of the content. The term is also used to refer to information on the internet that can be seen by users, as opposed to programming and other background information.

Cookie A cookie is a nugget of information sometimes sent by websites to your hard drive when you visit.They contain such details as what you looked at, what you ordered, and can add more information, so that the website can be customized to suit you.

Cybercafe Cafe where you can use a computer terminal to browse the net for a small fee.

Cyberspace When first coined by the sci-fi author William Gibson, it meant a shared hallucination which occured when people logged on to computer networks. Now, it refers to the virtual space you're in when on the internet.

D

Dial Up A temporary telephone connection to your ISP's computer and how you make contact with your ISP, each time you log onto the Internet.

Domain The part of an Internet address which identifies an individual computer, and can often be a business or person's name. For example, in the goodwebguide.com the domain name is theGoodWebGuide.

Download Transfer of information from an Internet server to your computer.

Dynamic HTML The most recent version of the HTML standard.

E

Ecash Electronic cash, used to make transactions on the internet.

Ecommerce The name for business which is carried out over the internet.

Email Mail which is delivered electronically over the internet. They are usually comprised of text messages, but can contain illustrations, music and animations. Mail is sent to an email address, which is the internet equivalent of a postal address.

Encryption A process whereby information is scrambled to produce a 'coded message', so that it can't be read whilst in transit on the internet. The recipient must have decryption software in order to read the message.

Expire Term referring to newsgroup postings which are automatically deleted after a fixed period of time.

Ezine Publication on the web, which is updated regularly.

F

FAQ Stands for frequently asked questions and is a common section on websites where the most common enquiries and their answers are archived.

Frame A method which splits web pages into several windows.

FTP/File Transfer Protocol Standard method for transporting files across the internet.

G

GIF/Graphics Interchange Format A format in which graphics are compressed, and a popular method of putting images onto the internet, as they take little time to download.

Gopher The gopher was the precursor of the world wide web and consisted of archives accessed through a menu, usually organised by subject.

GUI/Graphical User Interface. This is the system which turns binary information into the words and images format you can see on your computer screen. For example, instead of seeing the computer language which denotes the presence of your toolbar, you actually see a toolbar.

H

Hackers A term used to refer to expert programmers who used their skills to break into computer systems, just for the fun of it. Nowadays the word is more commonly associated with computer criminals, or Crackers.

Header Basic indication of what's in an email: who it's from, when it was sent, and what it's about.

Hit When a file is downloaded from a website it is referred to as a 'hit'. Measuring the number of hits is a rough method of counting how many people visit a website. Except that it's not wholly accurate as one website can contain many files, so one visit by an individual may generate several hits.

Homepage Most usually associated with a personal site, produced by an individual, but can also refer to the first page on your browser, or the first page of a website.

Host Computer on which a website is stored. A host computer may store several websites, and usually has a fast powerful connection to the internet. Also known as a Server.

HTML/Hypertext Mark-Up Language The computer code used to construct web pages.

HTTP/Hypertext Transfer Protocol The protocol for moving HTML files across the web.

Hyperlink A word or graphic formatted so that when you click on it, you move from one area to another. See also hypertext.

Hypertext Text within a document which is formatted so it acts as a link from one page to another, or from one document to another.

I

Image Map A graphic which contains hyperlinks.

Interface What you actually see on the computer screen.

Internet One or more computers connected to one another is an internet (lower case i). The Internet is the biggest of all the internets. and consists of a worldwide collection of interconnected computer networks.

Internet Explorer One of the most popular pieces of browser software, produced by Microsoft.

Internet Relay Chat See Chat.

Intranet A network of computers, which works in the same way as an internet, but for internal use, such as within a corporation.

ISDN/Integrated Services Digital Network Digital telephone line which facilitates very fast connections and can transfer larges amounts of data. It can carry more than one form of data at once.

ISP/Internet Service Provider See Access Provider.

J

Java Programming language which can be used to create interactive multimedia effects on webpages. The language is used to create programmes known as *applets* that add features such as animations, sound and even games to websites.

Javascript A scripting language which, like Java, can be used to add extra multimedia features. However, in contrast with Java it does not consist of separate programmes. Javascript is embedded into the HTML text and can interpreted by the browser, provided that the user has a javascript enabled browser.

JPEG Stands for 'Joint Photographic Experts Group' and is the name given to a type of format which compresses photos, so that they can be seen on the web.

K

Kill file A function which allows a user to block incoming information from unwanted sources. Normally used on email and newsreaders.

L

LAN/Local Area Network A type of internet, but limited to a single area, such as an office.

Login The account name or password needed to access a computer system.

Link Connection between web pages, or one web document and another, which are accessed via formatted text and graphic.

M

Mailing List A discussion group which is associated with a website. Participants send their emails to the site, and it is copied and sent by the server to other individuals on the mailing list.

Modem A device for converting digital data into analogue signals for transmission along standard phone lines. The usual way for home users to connect to the internet or log into their email accounts. May be internal (built into the computer) or external (a desk-top box connected to the computer).

MP3 A compressed music file format, which has almost no loss of quality although the compression rate may be very high.

N

Netscape Popular browser, now owned by AOL.

Newbie Term for someone new to the Internet. Used perjoratively of newcomers to bulletin boards or chat, who commit the sin of asking obvious questions or failing to observe the netiquette.

Newsgroup Discussion group amongst Internet users who share a mutual interest. There are thousands of newsgroups covering every possible subject.

O

Offline Not connected to the internet via a telephone line.

Online Connected to the internet via a telephone line.

Offline Browsing A function of the browser software, which allows the user to download pages and read them whilst offline.

Online Service Provider Similar to an access provider, but provides addtional features such as live chat.

P

PDF/Portable Document Format A file format created by Adobe for offline reading of brochures, reports and other documents with complex graphic design, which can be read by anyone with Acrobat Reader.

Plug-in Piece of software which adds more functions (such as playing music or video) to another, larger software program.

POP3/Post Office Protocol An email protocol that allows you to pick up your mail from any location on the web.

Portal A website which offers many services, such as search engines, email and chat rooms, and to which people are likely to return to often . ISPs such as Yahoo and Alta Vista provide portal sites which are the first thing you see when you log on, and in theory act as gateways to the rest of the web.

Post/Posting Information sent to a usenet group, bulletin board, message board or by email.

PPP/Point to Point Protocol The agreed way of sending data over dial-up connections, so that the user's computer, the modem and the Internet Server can all recognise it. It is the protocol which allows you to get online.

Protocol Convention detailing a set of actions that computers in a network must follow so that they can understand one another.

Q

Query Request for specific information from a database.

R

RAM /Random Access Memory Your computer's short term memory.

Realplayer G2 A plug-in program that allows you to view video in real-time and listen to sound and which is becoming increasingly important for web use.

Router A computer program which acts as an interface between two networks, and decides how to route information.

S

Searchable Database A database on a website which allows the user to search for information, usually be keyword.

Search Engine Programs which enable web users to search for pages and sites using keywords. They are usually to be found on portal sites and browser homepages. Infoseek, Alta Vista and Lycos are some of the popular search engines.

Secure Transactions Information transfers which are encrypted so that only the sender and recipient have access to the uncoded message, so that the details within remain private. The term is most commonly used to refer to credit card transactions, although other information can be sent in a secure form.

Server A powerful computer that has a permanent fast connection to the internet. Such computers are usually owned by companies and act as host computers for websites.

Sign-on To connect to the internet and start using one of its facilities.

Shareware Software that doesn't have to be paid for or test version of software that the user can access for free, as a trial before buying it.

Standard A style which the whole of the computer industry has agreed upon. Industry standards mean that hardware and software produced by the various different computer companies will work with one another.

Surfing Slang for looking around the Internet, without any particular aim, following links from site to site.

T

TLA/Three Letter Acronyms Netspeak for the abbreviations of net jargon, such as BPS (Bits Per Second) and ISP (Internet Service Provider).

U

Upload To send files from your computer to another one on the internet. When you send an email you are uploading a file.

URL/Uniform Resource Locator Jargon for an address on the internet, such as www.thegoodwebguide.co.uk.

Usenet A network of newsgroups, which form a worldwide system, on which anyone can post 'news'.

V

Virtual Community Name given to a congregation of regular mailing list/ newsgroup users.

VRML/Virtual Reality Modeling Language Method for creating 3D environments on the web. On a

W

Wallpaper Description of the sometimes hectic background patterns which appear behind the text on some websites.

Web Based Email/Webmail Email accounts such as Hotmail and Rocketmail, which are accessed via an Internet browser, rather than an email program such as Outlook Express. Webmail has to be typed whilst the user is online, but can accessed from anywhere on the Web.

Webmaster A person responsible for a web server. May also be known as System Administrator.

Web Page Document which forms one part of a website (though some sites are a single page), usually formatted in HTML.

Web Ring Loose association of websites which are usually dedicated to the same subject and often contain links to one another.

Website A collection of related web pages which often belong to an individual or organisation and are about the same subject.

World Wide Web The part of the Internet which is easy to get around and see.The term is often mistakely interchanged with Internet, though the two are not the same. If the Internet is a shopping mall, with shops, depots, and delivery bays, then the web is the actual shops which the customers see and use.

Index

How to use your CD Rom

Now we've whetted your appetite for the sites reviewed in this book, we can help you to visit them quickly and easily. By registering on thegoodwebguide site, you will be able to use the hotlinks to all the sites listed, so you just click and go. You can also read the latest versions of reviews and see what we think of new sites that have been launched since the book went to press. If you wish, you can even have the updates emailed to you.

INSTALLATION INSTRUCTIONS FOR PC USERS

Insert the CD enclosed with this book into your CD drive of your PC. A welcome screen will appear with two buttons:

The goodwebguide button To register your purchase of a Good Web Guide book and to receive free updates of the reviews in the book and reviews of the latest sites, click on this button. When you've registered you can click straight through to any of the sites listed. You must have an internet connection to do this. If you are not already signed up with an internet service, you will need to install the LineOne software first.

If you click on the goodwebguide button you will be taken to a registration page where you will be asked to confirm which title in the series you have bought and to register your details. You then have free access to the updates of the website reviews in this book and to new reviews. You will also have access to the rest of the goodwebguide website.

LineOne button If you would like access to the internet you can click on this button to install LineOne's free ISP (internet service provider) software. You will need a modem to have internet access. If you already have an internet connection (ISP) you can still install LineOne as an alternative provider.

A To join LineOne just click on the LineOne button. When the first screen appears you have a choice: If you are a new user and wish to load Internet Explorer 5 as your browser, select 'Join Now'. On the next screen, select 'Go!' and you will be taken to the Microsoft installation process.

B To join immediately, without installing a browser, click 'Join Now' and then choose 'custom' to go straight to registration.

From the 'Welcome to LineOne' screen, click 'Go' and follow the on-screen instructions.

MAC USERS

This CD is not suitable for Apple Macintosh computers. For Free LineOne Mac Software call free on 0800 111 210.

RETURNING TO THE GOOD WEB GUIDE

Once you've connected to the internet, you can either type www.thegoodwebguide.co.uk into your browser to go directly to our website, or re-insert your CD and click on the goodwebguide button.

SUPPORT

If you have any problems, call the LineOne support number
CALL 0906 30 20 100
(calls may be monitored or recorded for training purposes)
24 hours, 365 days a year. Calls charged at 50p/minute or email support@lineone.net for free support.

Other titles in thegoodwebguide series include

Parents ISBN 1-903282-03-9

Gardening ISBN 1-903282-00-4

Money ISBN 1-903282-02-0

Food ISBN 1-903282-01-2

Forthcoming Good Web Guide titles

The Good Web Guide to Wine
ISBN 1-903282-04-7

The Good Web Guide to Travel
ISBN 1-903282-05-5

The Good Web Guide to Genealogy
ISBN 1-903282-06-3

The Good Web Guide to Health
ISBN 1-903282-08-X